7 PILLARS
DIGITAL MARKETING
FOR INSURANCE AGENCIES

THE BLUEPRINT FOR PROMOTING YOUR
AGENCY ONLINE AND DOMINATING YOUR MARKET

WEBSITE

CONTENT

EMAIL

THE
7 PILLARS
OF
DIGITAL
MARKETING

ADS

VIDEO

**SOCIAL
MEDIA**

REVIEWS

CHARLES & LINDA MUSSELWHITE

7 Pillars of Digital Marketing for Insurance Agencies

THE BLUEPRINT FOR PROMOTING YOUR AGENCY ONLINE AND DOMINATING YOUR MARKET

Charles & Linda Musselwhite

Musselwhite Consulting

ISBN: 0692291717
ISBN 13: 9780692291719
Library of Congress Control Number: 2016903875
Musselwhite Consulting, Temecula, CA

TABLE OF CONTENTS

Foreword

My name is Mike Stromsoe, and I am honored to introduce you to my friends Charles and Linda Musselwhite, the owners of Musselwhite Marketing and Consulting and the authors of two books, with this being the most recent.

As for me, I'll share a little bit about my own history. I am honored to be the president and team leader of Stromsoe Insurance Agency, a very proactive and dynamic independent insurance agency. Our **Total Protection Team** teaches families and businesses how to properly protect everything they work so hard for.

Owning and operating an independent insurance agency that grew from zero revenue to $1 million in less than nine years was an incredible journey. Now licensed in thirty-one states, we affectionately refer to our culture as the **"Living Agency Laboratory."** Our team continually refines and brings to market *only* tools that work. Our goal is to be a premier independent agency. I'm also the author of five books on various types of insurance and business matters, a keynote and national speaker on various insurance matters, a certified workers' compensation advisor, and the founder of the **Unstoppable Profit Producer Program**. I've been featured on Fox News as a special insurance correspondent and Access to Experts and interviewed on ESPN radio concerning marketing prowess in an insurance agency business. Simply put, our goal is to be a premier Independent Agency. I don't share all of this to brag or boast but to let you know I have an idea of what it takes to create a strong and profitable agency.

With our "The Unstoppable Profit Producer" program, we focus on changing the lives of business owners and helping them to create revolutionary results, all through a unique philosophy developed over twenty-nine years of research called the **three *P*s—People, Processes and Promotion**. We've created unique tools that any agent or business owner can immediately implement in over sixty-nine specific areas of business covering a variety of marketing and business building topics. As someone with a lifelong interest in marketing, I have invested thousands of hours and dollars for our agency to stay current and relevant in an ever-changing market. When it comes to online or digital marketing, most folks in the insurance industry find it challenging just to keep up. My encouragement to you is to find a partner who plays at the stuff you work at.

We all know there are lots of people calling themselves social media experts or Internet marketing consultants online these days. Unfortunately few of these folks understand our industry, business, prospects, and customers enough to deliver value that drives progress and return on investment. But I've been pleased to work with Linda and Charles Musselwhite for years, watching their expertise and client references grow all the while. I first met Linda and Charles in 2003 when they were starting their financial planning agency. I've been consistently impressed by their energy, creativity, and follow-through. You can get a taste of their Internet marketing expertise in this book the **"7-Pillars of Digital Marketing for Insurance Agencies."** Remember, they were once one of us, working in our business, and they understand what we do.

In *the 7-Pillars of Digital Marketing*, Linda and Charles go into detail about the things every insurance agency, agent, and broker should do to build a strong foundation of online marketing assets, including: (1) creating a website, (2) developing content, (3) sending e-mails, (4) creating videos, (5) running online ads, (6) social media promotion, and (7) generating reviews and testimonials.

I often say that "I've been there, done that, and *I'm still doing it.*" I have my own internal world-class marketing department, but I keep Charles and Linda on speed dial, because like me they are students of marketing and work hard to stay up on all the things online that me and my team have to work at. Linda and Charles make online marketing look like effortless play.

Throughout the book, Linda and Charles share tried-and-true marketing strategies and tips on targeting your audience, using social media, posting online ads, SEO, setting up e-mail marketing, and more. These tips can help you reduce the distraction (and expense) caused by all the "gurus" pitching "shiny objects" that target insurance agencies like yours and mine these days. This book cuts right to the chase, offering money and time-saving tips from the beginning.

The Musselwhites' practical, down-to-earth marketing strategies can help your business succeed.

If you have any questions about Linda and Charles Musselwhite, don't hesitate to contact me.

—Mike Stromsoe
Murrieta 2016

http://www.siaonline.com

http://www.unstoppableprofitproducer.com

INTRODUCTION

L et's face it: even though most adult Americans have insurable inter-ests like health, home, and automobile, just to name a few. The fact is most people don't wake up excited for the opportunity to discuss their insurance needs and pay (a premium) for something they hope they never have to use.

Today's insurance consumers are growing more finicky by the day. Most people don't want to schedule an appointment and go into an office. We're betting you've experienced a drop in foot traffic over the years that corroborates our opinion. To meet the market's desire for convenience, some enterprise-level agencies with deep pocket funds have spent millions of dollars on websites and software making it "click-simple" easy for almost anyone to log on, enter a little data, and use his or her credit card or even PayPal to buy coverage on line.

Today independent insurance agencies and brokers are finding suc-cessful marketing increasingly challenging. We talk to insurance agencies all the time and hear the same things over and over again:

- "Our phones aren't ringing anymore."
- "Our direct mail isn't as effective as it used to be."
- "We don't have any foot traffic."
- "We don't have to do marketing."
- "We don't understand website SEO."

- "We can't keep up with social media."
- And on and on.

A partial goal of marketing for any insurance agency is explaining how your product(s), service(s), and company are different from all the rest. A primary challenge in the insurance industry is that from company to company the financial products and services offered are essentially the same. So when marketing your products, your services, and your agency, you must dig deeper for creative ways to separate yourself from your competition. Deliberately and intentionally sharing positives about your company's reputation, the success of your products, and the testimonials of satisfied customers is a way to give you, your agency, and your financial products an edge in the marketplace.

Defining who you are as a company, what you're all about, and how you're different is a very subjective exercise requiring specific conversations about where your business is right now, where you want it to be, who your target audience(s) is, and so on. While this exercise is something that our team is very good at doing, it would be challenging at best for us to describe in a valuable and meaningful way how you should do this for your agency in the one-way conversation of this book.

We wrote *"The 7-Pillars of Digital Marketing"* to focus on the objective side of marketing your agency. It's our experience that most agencies aren't organized (enough) in their marketing, either don't have all the pieces or have too many pieces in their marketing puzzle to be effective, or are simply just not able to execute their marketing plan consistently (daily) enough.

Today whether we're shopping for tires for the car, a gym membership, or that once in a lifetime anniversary trip to Fiji, or insurance products the Internet has changed how we decide what to buy. Google, calls this online decision-making moment the **"Zero Moment of Truth"** — or simply ZMOT. Because of this, it is exponentially more profitable to be found when someone is **"searching"** for your products and services (the zero moment of truth), we provide you with a summary blueprint of the components needed to increase and improve your agency's online visibility and searchability in the following chapters.

Of all the workshops, webinars, and client work we've done over the years, **The 7-Pillars of Digital Marketing** described in this book has been our common method of success.

Unlike most books you've read, *The 7- Pillars of Digital Marketing* doesn't require that you read the chapters in sequential order. You can turn directly to the chapters and topics that appeal to you and focus only on the area(s) you are most interested in.

Before we jump in to the book, however, our mentors (those we've hired and those we've read) have impressed upon us to always underpromise and overdeliver, so, we're starting with a bonus right out of the chute!

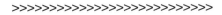

Click (or enter) the link below to receive a great bonus:

Online Marketing Kick-Start Tips
http://www.musselwhitemarketing.com/online-marketing-tips-kickstart

>>>>>>>>>>>>>>>>>>>>>>>>>>>>>>>

Important - Read This:

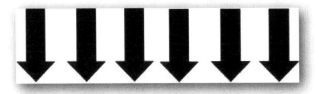

There are a lot of links to articles, posts, and other resources in this book. Whether you're reading the online version, the soft copy, or the hard copy, we've included all the links in the back of this book in the resource section.

Why Digital Marketing Is the Right Tool for Your Insurance Agency

Since you're reading this book, we bet you'd agree that digital marketing is growing at an accelerating rate. If you have an insurance agency today, digital marketing is mandatory.

If you choose to ignore digital marketing in your agency, you will get run over by those agencies and forward-thinking agents that embrace and leverage digital marketing technology and all it has to offer. They are the ones creating enhanced and improved user experiences as well as increased and improved efficiencies in their agencies.

But digital marketing and technology are not the be all, end all to online success. Digital marketing and technology are important and you must stay up on the rules for what's working, what isn't, and what's coming up, but you must also know (intimately) what your target audience wants. Marketing and technology without a great user experience still misses the mark and will cause you to work harder and still lose opportunities.

Man or woman, young or old, there currently exists a generation of digital consumers that have grown up online which marketers and insurance agencies have never before had to consider… **The Online Connected Generation**.

The Online Connected Generation is loosely defined as the group of consumers willing to communicate, build relationships, and ultimately make buying decisions using digital and social media tools which today can be anyone from the millennials to octogenarians and older.

So, no matter whether your prospects or clients were born in 1991 or 1941, whether they use digital and/or social media tools to communicate, whether or not they build relationships and ultimately make buying decisions, they are still part of The Online Connected Generation. According to Ad Age (Carmichael, Matt. "Marketing wasteland Clermont, Fla., May 28, 2012), "every day for the next two decades, 10,000 baby boomers will join in the marketing wasteland of 'seniors.' Add that to Gen X and Millennials demographics that seemed to have been born with technology and social media in their blood and it isn't hard to see that at the very least, insurance agencies need to start embracing and understanding digital and social media marketing."

The Online Connected Generation is Why We Use Digital Marketing

When age doesn't matter:

- You can focus less on demographic bias and more on who your consumers actually are.
- You don't have to hack up your marketing efforts to reach market segments.
- You can apply laser focus on the tools necessary to deliver your message.

The Online Connected Generation is why we use digital marketing tools such as websites, e-mail marketing, content marketing, video marketing, social media marketing, and online reviews and testimonials to help grow our clients businesses and ours.

However, what really attracts the Online Connected Generation is what others are saying about you on and off line and the experience they receive working with your agency.

The Customer Experience

What baby boomers, gen x-ers, gen y-ers, and millennials all want is the same thing that the older generation wants—a relationship. After all, we don't do business with businesses. We do business with people!

To begin building this relationship, you've got to focus on two critical pieces of the online success formula:

1. What the tech (Google, Bing, Yahoo, Facebook, YouTube, etc...) want from us so that we show up in people's search results?
2. What do our target audiences want from us after the search engines lead them to our sites and profiles for potential solutions to the problem(s) they are trying to solve?

Today, if you want to gain more web traffic (and make your phone ring), there are two primary ways to generate it: *search engine optimization* and *online ads*.

No joke; really, it's that easy! But hold on, it's easier said than done. This is true especially when you compare Google and all the other search engines (Bing, Yahoo, etc....) and look at over two hundred different factors to determine rank. Rank is the position at which your site appears in the search results. If you want more traffic on your site and your phone to ring, the following the *7-Pillars checklist* will ensure that you're enhancing your virtual footprint and digital marketing efforts.

When it comes to increasing and improving your online visibility and searchability, attention must be given to two distinct areas: **user experience** and **technical requirements**.

User experience is critical because if what you're doing turns off the very people you're trying to attract, it doesn't matter how good your tech is. The technical aspects are equally as important because if people are searching online for your products or services, you need to have done the right things so that they can find you online.

In this book, we'll look at both perspectives and what you can do to stack the deck in your favor.

As we've said before, "there are 7-Pillars to Digital Marketing":

1. Your website
2. Your content marketing
3. Your e-mail marketing
4. Your online advertising
5. Your video marketing
6. Your social media marketing
7. Your social credibility through reviews and testimonials

PILLAR #1

YOUR INSURANCE AGENCY WEBSITE

T oday your website is probably your most important digital asset. Your websites importance is grounded in two separate yet complimentary areas; user experience and technical requirements. Because of this, we spend a significant amount of time and space addressing a few of the more important items concerning your website.

Simply put, it is mandatory to have a business website representing your insurance agency. Your website acts as your virtual storefront, your online brick and mortar on the web. It is often the first impression a prospect will get of you and your agency. Your website is your virtual footprint and its importance has never been higher that it is at the present time and will probably continue to increase.

What Type of Website Should I Create?

Let's be honest: Not all insurance agency websites are the same. Some marketing agencies promote template sites that exclusively focus on insurance and offer hassle-free, speedy, and efficient website management but also come with some constraints concerning what you can and can't do.

There are template websites and there are custom sites, and there is everything in between. Regardless of the platform, your website should be an online university for your clients and prospects.

When it comes to prospects, your website *must* provide different ways of capturing visitor info (name and e-mail at a minimum) with different types of **"Calls-To-Action"** (CTA's) using different **lead magnets**. We'll get deeper into what all this means in the following sections.

Regardless of what type of website you select one thing is clear, change (internal and external) is inevitable. The website you choose today may not serve you well tomorrow and probably won't in a year or two. If you're still using the same website platform and layout three or more years from today we can almost guarantee you'll be losing traffic and opportunities! It's just the nature of online digital properties.

Duplicate Content Challenges

One potential drawback to using a niche-oriented website provider that we see too often is the repeated use of the same content template. While they may change the logos, pictures, names, addresses, and phone numbers to match your individual agency, they often also use duplicate content, which can cause ranking problems and possibly penalties.

But don't take our word for it—check out some of the articles addressing the problem written by reputable and authoritative names like Google, Yoast, Raven Tools, Search Engine Land, SEO Round Table, SEO SiteCheckup and MOZ:

- **Google Search Console Help**
- **Yoast Duplicate Content: Causes and Solutions**
- **Raven Tools: 10 Duplicate Content Scenarios and How to Solve Them**
- **Search Engine Land: 29% of Sites Face Duplicate Content Issues**

- **Search Engine Roundtable: How Do You Detect Duplicate Content Issues**
- **SEO SiteCheckup: The Truth About Duplicate Content Issues**
- **MOZ: What is Duplicate Content**

On many occasions we've seen firsthand duplicate content causing challenges. One case in particular still jumps out at us. (The names and locations have been changed to protect the innocent and unknowing.)

After we presented a webinar on **video marketing,** we were contacted by a Midwest insurance company with two locations that was soon to open a third. Their business was strong and growing. Although the agency's owner/broker was initially interested in video marketing, our conversation eventually focused on his websites. What we discovered was that his web developer copied his first website to use for his second, simply changing the address and phone number on their second website and was planning to do the same for their third.

What Google Thinks of Duplicate Content

Due to a number of factors, our suggestion in this situation would have been to build one website and add specific elements (header, footers, sidebars, pages, etc...) highlighting and differentiating each location for each. Because Google states there is *no* duplicate content penalty, some webmasters think that reusing content is not a problem, yet rankings can be impacted negatively by what seems to be duplicate content problems. And that's what was happening here. The agency wasn't being penalized but the other (duplicate) sites simply wouldn't rank well due to the duplicate content identification.

According to Google, (https://support.google.com/webmasters/answer/66359?hl=en) *duplicate content* "generally refers to substantive blocks of content within or across domains that either completely match other content or are appreciably similar. Mostly, this is not deceptive in origin."

Unfortunately if Google classifies your content as duplicate, thin, or boiler-plate content, then you probably have a major issue to deal with.

Duplicate, thin, or boiler-plate content violates Google's website performance recommendations, and if caught can be a very tedious and time consuming chore that will have to be resolved.

Keep in mind, Google uses bots to track down duplicate, thin, or boiler-plate content automatically. If you republish posts, press releases, news stories, or product descriptions found on other sites (yours or someone else's), your page and website ranking can (probably will) drop. By the way, Wikipedia defines (https://en.wikipedia.org/wiki/Internet_bot) an **Internet bot**, also known as **web robot**, **WWW robot** or simply **bot**, is a software application that runs automated tasks (scripts) over the Internet. Typically, bots perform tasks that are both simple and structurally repetitive, at a much higher rate than would be possible for a human alone. The largest use of bots is in web spidering (*web crawler*), in which an automated script fetches, analyzes and files information from web servers at many times the speed of a human.

Even though Google doesn't like using the word "penalty," if your site is made up entirely of republished content, you will have an extremely difficult time getting your page(s) or site to rank in Google and show up in any Google search engine results.

Remember, if you have multiple websites (a lot of insurance agencies we talked to do) selling the same products or services, you are going to cause more harm than good and drive your website traffic into the ground in the long run, rather than dominate your local niche.

You would save your agency money, management time, aggravation, and the headache of unwinding the issues created by all the duplicate content simply by not using it.

The Importance of Mobile Optimization

We'll go into more detail later, but basically mobile optimization (or, even better, "mobile responsiveness") for the proliferation of smart devices (smart phones, iPads, tablets, etc...) is an important factor in website design and function today. Stated frankly, your agency website should be mobile optimized ("responsive" even better).

This necessity of having a mobile-optimized or responsive website becomes crystal clear when you consider that **80 percent of Internet users** *use smart phones* to search the web. A much smaller (but quickly growing) percentage—**9 percent—are using smart watches** to search the web, according to the folks at Marketingland. Basically, if you want clients and prospects to find and visit your website you've got to make it easy for them. Studies have shown most users will leave a website if it is too difficult to use on their preferred device and then never come back.

Instead of risking alienating your online visitors, your time, effort and arguably money should give some focus to deliberately and intentionally providing your online visitors with easy ways to find and connect with your agency through a social media presence, implementing online advertising campaigns and establishing word of mouth recommendations via reviews and testimonials.

What this all suggests is that if you want your website to be found by folks looking for your insurance solutions (home owners, life, auto, RVs, business, etc…), you need an online presence—period. With a strong online presence, it is possible for people all over the world (especially your own backyard) to learn more about you, your services and the products you offer. As your virtual storefront, website visitors and prospects (future customers even) will know how to contact you. Done correctly, a website presence can position you above the competition and signal that you're the authoritative real deal for the consumer.

Having a website for your insurance agency has become standard practice. Websites are no longer something that insurance agencies merely should have; customers expect them. Websites and even an active social media presence can build credibility for you and your agency, especially if your site is updated frequently or you're consistently posting to sites like Facebook, YouTube, LinkedIn, or whatever platform your prospects use.

Now we're going to turn our attention to your agency website and the things you should be doing to improve technical requirements and user engagement to increase the certainty of being found at the right time (during a search - ZMOT) by the right person (someone searching).

We're going to cover some of the technical aspects of website SEO and suggest that if it gets too technical, you can feel free to skip ahead to another section. Just realize website SEO isn't something you do once or can simply ignore and hope it goes away or is solved through other efforts. Without a proper SEO strategy and tactics, all the other work you do or invest in won't provide you with the full ROI potential, because some folks simply won't find your website and therefore won't be able to consider and compare it to all the other websites they come across.

Maximizing Your Website SEO for Increased and Improved Online Visibility and Search Results

SEO, or search engine optimization, is comprised of two parts: on page and off page. *On-page SEO* involves the different parts of your website's pages (e.g., keywords, page content, meta descriptions, title tags, headings, image alt text, internal links, etc…).

Off-page SEO focuses more on promoting your content outside of your webpage (e.g., link building, social media, content, etc…). In this book we cover on-page SEO.

In our experience, improving the SEO of your insurance agency's website is one of the easiest (yet most time consuming) ways to improve and increase your online visibility and search results and will earn you way more traffic than what you're getting right now. Our first suggestion is to simply hire a reputable company to do your SEO for you. In our opinion, while SEO is a necessary component of the search success of your website, it usually takes too long for individuals to learn to do well and changes so fast that you're better off simply investing in the services of others to do it for you to accelerate this success metric in your business.

We use several tools to analyze websites for SEO. **WooRank** is an online software service providing small businesses, online marketers and SEO's with a solution to optimizing, promoting and measuring the effectiveness of their SEO free (or fee) of charge.

Thanks to our friends and partners at WooRank we've been given express permission from **Sam Gooch**, Head of Marketing at WooRank to share content about search engine optimization (and more) from their website and SEO reports throughout this book.

We use (and suggest you do too) WooRank software because it allows us in real-time to generate instant website reviews consisting of over 70 criteria to instantly spot and address critical website issues. As certified experts, WooRank is one of our favorite SEO tools.

WooRank offers *free* and *fee* versions of their online SEO report. While our team uses the fee version, we encourage you to visit the WooRank site and check out the free report for your website.

The full (fee) version of the WooRank online SEO report covers:

Title tags: technically known as title elements—define the title of a document, page or post. Title tags are often used on search engine results pages (SERPs) to display preview snippets for a given page. There are two things a good title must achieve:

1. Rank for your specific keywords
2. Make someone want to click on your page

Web page titles are critical to both user experience and search engine optimization. It creates value in three specific areas: relevancy, browsing, and in the search engine results pages.

Ideally, your title tag should contain between ten and seventy characters (spaces included). Make sure your title is explicit and contains your most important keywords optimized for searches and click-throughs (CTR). Be sure that each page has a unique title and only one <h1> tag per page/post (a tag is automatically assigned as your page/post title if you're using WordPress).

Your website should identify and discuss all the lines of coverage your agency offers. The title tag <h1> for each of these pages should generally be something like "The Top Five Reasons Why You Need Business Continuity Insurance in [name of your city or state] along with a complimentary meta title such as "The Top Five Reasons Why You Need Business Continuity Insurance."

You don't want to waste any pixels in your meta title (it should be fifty-five characters max), and putting your brand name in it (if room is available) is a great way to extend the length of your meta title while increasing the amount of CTR.

Meta descriptions: Ideally, your meta description should contain between 70 and 160 characters (spaces included). Yes, meta descriptions still matter in that they allow you to influence how your web pages are described and displayed in search results.

It is important to ensure that each of your web pages has a unique meta description that is explicit and contains your most important keywords for each page (these appear in bold when they match part or all of the user's search query). Good meta descriptions act in similar fashion to organic advertisements encouraging viewers to click through to your site to learn more.

To monitor the health of your website make sure to check your Google Search Console (Search Appearance > HTML Improvements) for any warning messages or notifications about your sites meta descriptions being too long or short or duplicated across more than one page.

Heading tags: Are a series of html elements that define the importance of the text on the webpage. Also known a HTML header tags, head tags, heading tags, h tags, and SEO header tags they are used to differentiate the heading of a page from the rest of the content.

There are six header tags, ranging from H1 to H6. H1 tags carry the most importance and authority while the least important is the H6 tag. There should be only one h1 tag per page while there can be multiple H2 – H6 tags. In HTML, the header tags from h1 to h6 form a hierarchy, which means that if you skip any of the tag numbers (e.g., jump from <h1>

to <h3>) the heading structure will be broken, which is bad news for on-page SEO. So, spend a few extra minutes and review your <h2>—<h6> tags to make sure they are set up correctly.

Internal links: It's a good practice to link from page to page and post to post on your agency website. For instance, with a little thought and creativity, you can easily link the descriptions of your types of insurance coverage with other services by adding statements that address the importance of having complementary coverages. You might talk about the benefit and savings of multipolicy discounts and place anchor text links to homeowners, auto, life, and so on.

Not only do links enable users to discover more of your content, products, and services, and thereby help to keep them engaged on your site for longer; they also help Google to crawl and recrawl pages and posts that it may not have visited in a while. This may not seem all that important but we deliberately and intentionally use internal links liberally because website pages and will decline in search rankings if they haven't been visited by the Googlebot for a reasonable period of time.

External links: Contrary to popular opinion, linking to external sites with strong page rank is good for increasing and improving your online visibility and search results. If you're linking to relevant, high-quality posts and articles within your pages and posts, Google will see that you're a more reputable site since you're crediting other high-quality sources.

Linking to established sites like Wikipedia or affiliated industry partner agencies like Allied, Chubb, CAN, Employers, Foremost, Hartford, MetLife, Mercury and giving them a possible thumbs-up is doing things the right way.

Not only that but you're actually providing a great benefit to your readers. If your audience knows that you'll provide them with other great information whenever they need it, why wouldn't they keep coming back? They're getting more useful information for just the effort of visiting your site. And don't worry that you're going to lose them by linking away from your site. They will still need and want you to help bind their coverage.

Broken links: A single broken link may not seem like a big deal but a broken link can do serious damage to your site's usability, reputation, and SEO possibly resulting in lost customer and revenue. What do you do when experience a broken link? We're betting that the majority of time you navigate away from the page and the search unless it was something that was of major interest to you. The problem this creates is when visitors spend less time on your site, search engine algorithms assume it's because your site isn't providing them with quality content or information, resulting in a lower ranking.

Broken links are often caused by changes in file name or structure or when an external website has gone offline. It is important to check periodically (weekly/monthly) and make sure you don't have any broken links on your pages and posts. When you find broken links, take the time to replace or remove each one. Authenticating your agency's website with Google Search Console (formerly Webmaster Tools) is one of the best ways to understand how your site is perceived by Google. When Google encounters broken links on your site (aka "crawl errors"), you'll be notified through the Webmaster Tools dashboard.

You can also use online sites like Online Broken Link Checker, Dead Link Checker, or W3C Link Checker to analyze every page on your website and point you to any broken URLs that you may have. You can also search, find, and install "Broken Link Checker" plugins if you're using WordPress.

Once you have a list of dead links on your site, you should remove or update them wherever possible to show search engines (and users) that you stay on top of your content and don't cite irrelevant information.

Robots.txt: Stands for robots exclusion protocol, which simply means we're telling search engine robots and spiders how to crawl and index pages on your website. A robots.txt file allows you to restrict access to specific directories and pages for search engine robots that crawl the web. It also specifies where the XML sitemap file is located.

The Google Search Console (formerly Webmaster Tools) is a very robust and helpful tool for a myriad of reasons. You can use the Google

Search Console to check for errors in your robots.txt file by selecting Robots.txt Tester under Crawl. This also allows you to test individual pages to make sure that Googlebot has the appropriate access.

XML sitemap: Is really nothing more than a list of URL's for a site that are available for crawling by search engine robots and can include additional information like your site's latest updates, frequency of changes, and importance of linked URLs. The sitemap allows search engines to crawl the site more intelligently. It is also good practice to specify your sitemap's location in your robots.txt file.

It's important to note that you only want to include pages in your sitemap that you want search engines to crawl. Do not include any pages that you have blocked via your robots.txt file. Check the URLs you link to on your site to ensure that none of them causes a redirect or return error code. You also need to be consistent with how you write your URLs; for example, being regular about whether or not you precede the address with *www*, by including the correct protocol (*http* or *https*), and by making sure URLs all end with or without a trailing slash.

Domain registration: Because newer domains generally struggle to get indexed and to rank high in search results for their first few months (depending on other associated ranking factors), consider buying a second-hand domain name that has already attained this status.

You can register your domain for up to ten years. Doing so will show the world (and search engines) that you are serious about your business.

Image size: Having images on your insurance agency website is important to fulfill tech requirements and promote user engagement. Proper image implementation is often misunderstood and overlooked. With page load time becoming such an important metric in search and user experience, reducing the size of your images can increase and improve your online visibility and search results. Images are some of the largest files on your website. You can easily reduce the size of your images with online sites like Image Optimizer or Optimizilla or by using WordPress plugins such as WP Smush.it or EWWW Image Optimizer.

Quite often, these image compression tools allow you to reduce the size of your files by up to 90 percent!

Image alt tags: Staying on the theme of images, it is important to check the images on your website to make sure effective alternative text is specified for each. Your pictures should have descriptive alt tags. One the most prevalent SEO violations we see is that a lack of image alt tags. Although you can see your image on your own website, search engines only look at the code of these images. Adding alternative text to the image can help to reinforce how relevant a page is to its target keywords, while also making it more likely that the image will be displayed in the Google Images search results.

Not writing a description leaves these fields blank. Although you're not penalized for blank image alt tags, you're definitely not helped by them, either.

It takes five seconds to write something descriptive about your image and it allows search engines (Google) to understand what the image is all about. This simple action can help your agency website rank more highly and give you a boost in image searches, too. To optimize your website's page load times, restrict the number of characters in the alt text to 150, including spaces, and minimize the size of images.

In case you're wrestling to come up with a descriptive alt tag, the following example might help. Let's say you've got pictures of a home, an apartment, or a commercial truck on your website, a remarkably technical alt tag might be something like:

- "Homeowners Insurance—[your insurance agency's name]"
- "Renters Insurance—[your insurance agency's name]"
- "Commercial Auto Insurance—[your insurance agency's name]"

Keywords: it is important to be consistent with your use of keywords. To improve the chance of ranking well in search results, make sure you include your keyword in some or all of the following: page URL, page content, title tag, meta description, header tags, image alt attributes, internal link anchor text, and backlink anchor text.

Semantic keywords: We'll save you a boring and confusing dissertation on latent semantic indexing and just say it's a technique search engines use as they continue to get smarter to identify patterns in the relationships between the terms and concepts.

As search engines (Google, Bing Yahoo, etc.) get smarter (daily), they understand that certain words mean different things. They're so smart that you can use variations of keywords and get the same search juice.

Keyword stuffing: Is an outdated SEO technique that should be avoided, keyword stuffing refers to loading the meta tags or content on a web page with keywords. Keyword stuffing is to be avoided as it could lead to your website being banned or penalized in search ranking on major search engines. So again, it goes without saying that *this practice is to be avoided*!

So, if you're writing (or have written) a webpage or a post about the best auto coverages, you shouldn't keep trying to fit in the keyword "best auto coverages" throughout your content. Using semantic variations of the keyword once in the title and a couple of times on the page or in the post is more than enough.

Some examples of keyword variations include:

- "Best auto insurance coverage options"
- "What is the best auto insurance coverage to have?"
- "Auto coverages definitions"
- "Auto coverages explained"
- "Types of auto coverage"
- "Cheap auto insurance coverage"
- "Good auto insurance coverage"
- "Good auto insurance coverage amounts"

You're really only limited by your imagination of different ways to say the most. So mix it up a bit—variation is more enjoyable for a reader and Google knows this!

Word count: Search engines (especially Google) don't like thin pages or posts (consisting of less than five hundred words). If you want to establish yourself, both with Google and with a loyal audience, it's all about long-form content. This doesn't mean you have to keep writing and writing to hit a certain word count. If you've written a 950-word article that is high quality, that will be widely appreciated, and that couldn't be bettered by anyone else, then feel free to publish it.

However, we would say that *five hundred words is the minimum for an article* and suggest the more words the better, typically.

A lesser-known tactic involving word count is keeping your page ratios of text to HTML code *higher than 15 percent.* You can always improve your ratios by adding more text content to your pages. A good rule of thumb is to keep your text to HTML code ratio between 25 and 70 percent. Anything higher than 70% and your page or post runs the risk of being considered spam. Personally we feel the best practice is to focus on and write for the person (not the search engine) and the content is relevant and gives essential information.

A quick word on the importance of great content: Some very smart and successful marketers we know made the deliberate and intentional decision to not hire salespeople but rather to invest in the best content writers (for their websites, blog posts, e-mails, videos, and so on) whom they could afford. This strategy worked like gangbusters! This particular company doubled their business every year (for three years at this time of this report) and is generating well over $6 million a year without a traditional sales force.

If you're not a writer (it is not your fault—most people are not), we suggest investing in the services of the best content writer(s) you can afford. A good content writer knows what search engines are looking for and also takes user experience into account. Think of content not as a cost but as an investment.

In our own business, hiring writers was one of the best investments we made. Our writers have the training, experience, and skill to write faster, better, and more creatively than we ever could.

Indexed pages: This refers to the pages on your website that are indexed by search engines. Think of indexed pages as a library of your website pages on search engines. It is important to aim to have all of your web pages crawled and indexed by the search engines, as this gives you more opportunity for your website to be found. There are no absolutes when it comes to indexed pages, but generally speaking, more is always better.

A low number of indexed pages (relative to the total number of pages/URLs on your website) indicates that you have an issue, whether it is due to a bad internal linking structure or unknowingly preventing search engines from crawling your pages.

To resolve this, make sure your website has an XML sitemap and that you submit it to the major search engines using your Google Search Console account. Working to increase and improve your websites backlinks helps search engine bots discover, crawl, index, and rank your web pages, while building authority, diversity and relevancy.

Check Google Search Console under Google Index and Crawl to keep track of the status of your site's indexed/crawled pages.

Duplicate content: As we elaborated on before, duplicate content is a fast and growing problem! Duplicate content can lower your site's search engine rankings and reduce the traffic to your site. There are dozens of things that cause duplicate content. Most of them are technical, but the how and why aren't as important as detecting and fixing the problem.

You're likely to have more duplicate content on your site than you think! Duplicate content does not just apply to copied or slightly amended text from other websites; it can also be content that appears on multiple pages on your own site. As a best practice, make sure that you never have duplicate content anywhere on your site.

For example, if you use tags on your blog posts, those article(s) could appear under every one of those tag pages unless you deindex the tags using your robots.txt file. This may sound technical and/or confusing, but it's simple enough to do. Preventing search engines from indexing pages that have duplicate content on them, such as your tag pages and search results pages, reduces the risk of your content being devalued by search engines.

To find out if your site has any duplicate content, broken links, or other issues, you can visit sites like Siteliner, Copyscape, and PlagSpotter.

In-page links: While there is no exact limit to the number of links you should include on a webpage, the best practice is to avoid exceeding two hundred.

Even though links pass value from one page to another, the amount of value that can be passed is split between all of the links on a page. This means that adding unnecessary links will dilute the potential value attributed to the other links.

Using the Nofollow attribute prevents value from being passed to the linking page, but it is worth noting that these links are still taken into account when calculating the value that is passed between each link, so Nofollow links can also dilute page rank.

Load time: Site speed is an important factor for ranking high in Google search results and enriching the user experience.

According to websites like StatisticBrain and the National Center for Biotechnology Information, the average attention span of a human being has dropped from twelve seconds in 2000 to eight seconds in 2013. The latest figure is one second less than the attention span of a goldfish (who figures this stuff out). "Even incredibly patient people cannot stand waiting in lines—whether that is at a bank, airport, or restaurant. We either get bored or angry that it is taking longer than expected" (Costill, Albert. https://www.searchenginejournal.com/seo-101-important-site-speed-2014/111924 July 25, 2014).

From a user experience standpoint, if the page load time on your website is slow, that could be enough to make someone click away. From a techie (search engine) standpoint, poor user experience and slow website speed reduces search ranking. Faster load times will indeed improve your user experience and website ranking, which will help you gain more organic traffic.

To run a free speed test of your website visit PageSpeed Insights or WebPageTest.

Then, check out Google's developer tutorials for tips on how to make your website run faster. And to monitor your server and receive SMS alerts when your website is down, take a look at these website monitoring services:

- Uptime Robot
- Monitor.us
- Montastic
- Site24x7
- Service Uptime

PageSpeed Insights is a must-use tool from Google that gives you a page speed score and analyzes of both the desktop and mobile versions of your site. It will also give you recommendations that are divided into high, medium, or low priority.

Supported by Google, WebPageTest allows you to run a free website speed test. It provides charts that break down content, checks for page speed optimization, and makes suggestions for improvements after giving a page speed score out of one hundred.

Bounce rate: An important ranking factor, bounce rate is the percentage of visitors to your website who navigate away from your site after viewing only one page. A high or rising bounce rate is a sure sign that your home or landing page is boring or off-putting.

So, what is a good bounce rate? This is an extremely difficult question to answer, as bounce rate is heavily influenced by your industry and the type of site (blog, informational, entertainment, etc.). Two measures of a good bounce rate are whether the amount of visitors who leave the site is dropping and whether it is lower than that of your competitors.

There are several tools available to measure and track your website's bounce rate, but one of the best and easiest, Google Analytics, is free and simply requires an install. After that, get in the habit of reviewing and analyzing your site's bounce rate routinely.

Two easy ways to increase and improve your site's bounce rates, online visibility, and search results are to use clear calls to action (CTAs) on your landing pages to clear the navigation and to make sure your content is easy to read.

Your website's bounce rate is an important ranking factor that you should review monthly, and definitely no less than quarterly.

If you are into the technical geeky website ranking factors like we are and want to learn more, check out Brian Dean's article Google's 200 Ranking Factors: The Complete List.

Structured data markup: Is used by search engines to generate rich snippets in search engine results, which are those small bits of information under each search result. This structured data is added directly to a page's HTML markup and is a way for website owners to send structured data to search engine robots, helping them to understand their content and create well-presented search results.

Google supports a number of rich snippets for content types, including: Reviews, People, Products, Businesses and Organizations, Recipes, Events, Videos, and Music. If your website covers any of these topics, we suggest that you annotate it with Schema.org using microdata to take advantage of this extra search result real estate.

Backlinks: Serving as letters of recommendation for your site, backlinks are links on other websites that point to yours. There is no perfect number when it comes to backlinks, but generally speaking, more is always better.

Since having them is crucial to your SEO, you should have a strategy to improve the quantity and quality of backlinks.

Social shareability: Since the impact of social media can be huge for insurance agencies, it is important to make sure you have set up social media profiles on Facebook, Twitter, LinkedIn, Google+, and other sites that are of interest to your customers.

If you haven't already, we strongly suggest learning how to engage your social media audiences with valuable and informative content to create a strong and consistent fan base. Your goal is to use your website to increase your popularity on social platforms.

The following sites offer helpful tools for managing your social media campaigns:

- Hootsuite
- SproutSocial
- CrowdBooster

Increased and Improved Online Visibility and Search Results from Making Your Site Mobile Friendly

Users' mobile searches for insurance products and services are exploding! Just check out these stats:

- 61 percent of local searches on a mobile phone result in a phone call (Google, 2012).
- 91 percent of all smart phone users have their phone within arm's reach 24/7 (Morgan Stanley, 2012).
- 70 percent of all mobile searches result in action being taken in one hour. Seventy percent of online searches result in action being taken in one month (Mobile Marketer, 2012).
- Nine out of ten mobile searches lead to an action being taken, with over half leading to a purchase (Search Engine Land, 2012).

- Whereas it takes ninety minutes for the average person to respond to an e-mail, it takes ninety seconds for the average person to respond to a text message (CTIA.org, 2011).
- Mobile coupons get ten times the redemption rate of traditional coupons (Mobile Marketer, 2012).
- 44 percent of Facebook's one billion monthly users access Facebook on their phones. These people are twice as active while on Facebook as nonmobile users (Facebook, 2012).

With nearly four of five consumers conducting searches for a local business using smart phones or tablets, there are millions of people who are searching for companies like your insurance agency on their phone every single day. If you own a smart phone, we bet you have searched for a local company, too.

As of April 21, 2015, Google rolled out another significant algorithm change, expanding the use of mobile friendliness as a ranking signal. Google noted that this change would have more of an impact than Penguin or Panda!

You can check the mobile friendliness of your site by visiting the Google Developers Mobile-Friendly Test site. This site analyzes a URL and reports whether the pages have a mobile-friendly design.

When it comes to making your site mobile friendly, there are really two options: make it mobile friendly or make it responsive. A mobile site is essentially a copy of your website, for which the server does the work delivering an optimized webpage that is smaller and easier to navigate providing a customized unique experience for mobile users. A mobile site is a good choice for users that find it too expensive to redesign responsively. A reworking of your site for smartphones might be needed in order to stay current with next-generation phones and mobile browsers, typically requiring higher maintenance and expense.

Website using responsive design, allows the mobile device to do the work of sizing and moving website elements automatically according to a device's screen size (large or small) and orientation (landscape or portrait). It switches between these options on the fly. This is a very good and flexible solution and is more forward thinking because once you add it to your site, it will work on the coming month's and year's devices without having to be programmed further. It is a much better return on your investment in our opinion.

Some of the best and easiest tools we have found to make your website mobile compliant are:

- Duda
- Mobify
- Wirehernode
- Mippin
- Onbile
- Winksite
- Mofuse

If you are using WordPress for your insurance agency website, the following plug-ins can add mobile-friendly functionality to your site:

- **Jetpack:** gives site owners the mobile-friendly features of hosted wordpress.com with your self-hosted site.
- **WPTouch:** creates a separate, mobile-friendly version of your site.
- **WP Mobile Detector**: similarly to WPTouch, this plug-in provides some themes to present to visitors using a mobile device.

Wow, discussing websites was a lot to take on and truthfully we didn't even scratch the surface. It would be impossible in a book like this to address all the different website platforms, combinations of functionality, and overall website goals. For this reason, we strongly suggest that if you don't have in-house talent, you partner with an experienced webmaster or, better yet, an agency that will provide the required and necessary attention to your website that it needs and deserves. Remember, your website is your virtual storefront and may be the first experience someone has with your business.

Because search engine optimization can be tricky and frustrating, we've provided you with some other bonuses:

Local SEO Checklist
http://www.musselwhitemarketing.com/local-seo-checklist

Website design report
http://www.musselwhitemarketing.com/website-design-report

>>>>>>>>>>>>>>>>>>>>>>>>>>>>>>>>>>>>>>>

Important - Read This:

There are a lot of links to articles, posts, and other resources in this book. Whether you're reading the online version, the soft copy, or the hard copy, we've included all the links in the back of this book in the resource section.

PILLAR #2

CONTENT MARKETING FOR YOUR INSURANCE AGENCY

A website without content…well, we don't know what you would call it other than useless.

Content in the context of a website applies to all of the following:

- Keywords
- Page copy
- Blogs
- Calls to action
- e-mail
- e-books
- Regular books
- Video
- White papers

- Cheat sheets
- Reports
- etc...

Generally speaking, website content creation for your insurance agency is an *ongoing process* involving attracting and retaining customers by consistently **creating and curating relevant and valuable content and** integrating it into your overall marketing strategy.

Content marketing is the art and activity of consistently communicating with your customers and prospects in meaningful and valuable ways without trying to sell them products. It is noninterruptive marketing. The focus is on delivering educational information that makes your buyer more intelligent instead of pitching your coverages or services. The essence of this content strategy is simple: *Education is the new selling!* As businesses, when we focus on and deliver consistent and valuable information to buyers, we empower them with the info and data they need to make purchasing decisions. The goal of content marketing is to drive sales, fill the pipeline, and help your company grow.

Done correctly and consistently enough, content marketing offers value, separate from the products and services you sell. When you publish and promote content that is educational, entertaining, and useful to your audience, you will drive engagement, awareness, and ultimately sales for your agency.

So, what types of content can insurance agencies use to promote their companies?

- Blogs
- Social media postings
- e-newsletters
- Articles on your website
- In-person events
- Case studies

- Videos
- Photographs, illustrations, and other images
- White papers
- Online presentations
- Infographics
- Webinars/webcasts
- Podcasts
- Research reports
- Microsites

Most folks wrestle with keeping up with a consistent content marketing strategy (it's not your fault—we do, too!), which is why we hired a team to produce content for our business. One of the sayings we often share with business owners about content is "It is not an expense, it is an investment." Truer words than this could not be spoken, especially when it comes to the content marketing activities for your insurance agency. To get started, you could record a weekly vlog (video log), write a monthly blog, or simply come up with relevant topics for the next twelve to eighteen months and then give this task of content production to someone else so that you can focus on higher-level revenue-producing activities.

Keep in mind that your agency will not reach the million-dollar status if you are constantly doing $50 an hour work! *Delegate*!

One cool side benefit of hiring a content marketer is the automatic creation and publication of content that can be referred to, modified, reused, and repurposed over time.

Regardless of your industry or company size, a blog should be the hub of your content-marketing efforts. According to the folks at Content Marketing Institute, the most effective marketers use social media more than any other tactic; on average, the most successful companies use an average of seven social media platforms. According to the research, LinkedIn is both the most popular and the most effective site for content promotion for business-to-business marketing.

When it comes to insurance products, we bet you would agree that most prospects and customers do not understand them. As a matter of fact, you probably think that most folks do not want to purchase or even use them, right?

But think about it: insurance encroaches on just about everything people value:

- Homeowner insurance is about the people's most valued possessions.
- Auto insurance is about mobility.
- Life insurance is more about the financial security of the insured's family than it is about the insured.

These are things people care about and want to protect—they do not think about them once a year; they think about them every single day. But the insurance industry on the whole is failing to take advantage of its unique ability to be an integral part of the ongoing conversations surrounding these areas. Because of this, there is a huge opportunity for you to develop, launch, and refine your agency's content marketing program(s).

In our opinion a lot of folks in the insurance industry do not truly understand their buyers' personas and journeys. This becomes especially apparent when we hear and see their marketing ideas, strategies, and tactics.

Bottom line is that to be a successful insurer you must rethink and take control of your customer's relationships with new offerings, new capabilities, and optimized channels.

So, what kind of conversation do insurance consumers want?

One of most prolific marketers of all time is Dan Kennedy. This is the man who introduced us to the concept of "swipe and deploy." The swipe and deploy concept simply involves looking for a company that has the audience or type of audience you want and mimicking their efforts. The idea is not that you should copy, steal, or plagiarize what they are doing; it is study what they are doing and create your own collateral.

The type of content we see being shared by the most successful insurance agencies on social media, more than any other, are things like local events, hints, tips, and advice.

People share content for different reasons, but offering help is one of the more common. When people find helpful advice, they are likely to share it with friends, neighbors, and family. At the other end of the spectrum, the least-shared content, unsurprisingly, is product information.

Although most people need homeowner's insurance to protect their biggest financial asset, what they really want to know is how to protect and increase the value of their home. They want to avoid water damage from failed pipes as well learn about the best home improvement investments. They want to avoid mold and termite damage and help choosing the bathroom or kitchen remodel. They want to avoid conditions that could cause fire damage or worse.

Insurance helps policy owners cope with disasters, but they also want to know how to avoid them in the first place. They want to know how to teach their kids how to be safer drivers, how to live healthier lives, and even whether to accept that pesky rental car insurance when on vacation.

People might not understand insurance policies, but they understand and value the things that insurance protects. The conversation often revolves around how *to avoid* having to use insurance policies.

In our opinion, social media "shares" are more powerful than "likes," because a share means someone is introducing/endorsing your blog, your company, your products/services, or *you* to someone that might not know who you are, what you do, or how you can help.

Offering ongoing hints, tips, and advice is also a powerful way to connect with today's consumers who are choosing products and the suppliers that are providing them. Through content curation this becomes an easier and less time consuming activity allowing you to provide advice from a number of experts and accumulate information from a variety of sources over a period of time. The ability to deliver information through the trusted medium of friends and family increases its perceived value significantly.

The common thread with successful content is not just its relevance to the community but that the community contributes to it. The community has much to add and share, especially when they tell their personal stories, which vastly enhances the value of any campaign.

Insurance has changed very little; it has always been built around the concept of expert advisors armed with facts. Advisors remain important, because people still value interaction with a person at the point of purchase. But the point of purchase is just one moment in the customer's journey.

Increasingly, insurance agents and brokers are turning to content curation to engage clients and prospects on social media. Social media-savvy agents and brokers are tracking content on sites that cover auto, life, home, health, and business insurance; selecting and commenting on relevant content; and sharing their links. People benefit from quality content that is prefiltered and put into context by a professional.

One of the most important elements of online marketing is custom content. When done correctly, custom content improves the readability of your website and helps to optimize it for search engines. This content needs to be unique to your agency in order to differentiate you from the competition. Using it can improve the time visitors spend on your website and help with customer acquisition and retention.

One of our favorite content-marketing strategies is the use of lead magnets. A lead magnet is basically a useful feature that your agency can offer as an ethical bribe on your home page or landing page to incentivize potential customers to give you their name, e-mail, phone number, address, or whatever info you are asking for.

Eleven Different Kinds of Lead Magnets

1. A video course that can be accessed all at once
2. A video course delivered via autoresponder, over a 5 day period (we will discuss videos more in pillar #5)
3. An infographic so useful browsers will want to tape it to their refrigerator or their office wall
4. A home maintenance calendar
5. A checklist for how to do something that needs to be done more than once, or that seems complicated
6. Cheat sheets, flow charts, or process charts
7. A how-to e-book in PDF format
8. Coupons to other local businesses for discounts, for free shipping, or even a free cup of coffee...you get the idea.
9. Free tickets to a special event (best for local businesses)
10. Giveaways or contests or sweepstakes people can sign up for
11. Access to a live webinar, a recorded webinar, or workshop (or any other audio file)

Need more ideas on what to write about on your site? The following resources cover a wide array of topics with knowledgeable information and perspectives. Check them out to generate ideas and articles for the content on your website.

Finance Sites and Blogs

- CNN Money
- Daily Finance
- Bank Rate
- Main Street
- SmartMoney
- Kiplinger
- Motley Fool

News Sites and Blogs

- *Financial Times*
- *New York Times*—"Your Money" section
- *New York Times*—"Health" section
- *Wall Street Journal—Health* blog
- Time—Healthland

Nonprofit Sites and Blogs

- National Association of Insurance Commissioners
- Insurance Information Institute
- The Life & Health Insurance Foundation for Education
- HealthCare.Gov Blog
- National Institutes of Health
- National Highway Safety Traffic Administration
- Insurance Institute For Highway Safety
- AAA Safety News

Industry Sites and Blogs

- Insurance Journal
- Property Casualty 360 Risk
- Property Casualty 360 Claims
- Business Insurance
- Life Health Pro
- Claims Journal
- Risk and Insurance
- About.com—Business Insurance
- About.com—Insurance
- Workers Comp Insider
- Winzer Insurance
- Consumer Insurance Blog

Content marketing can truly be an amazing tool that serves two purposes in your marketing arsenal. First, it helps search engines understand what you, your website, your products and services, and your business are all about so that they can provide increased and improved search engine results for your site.

Second, it provides prospects and future clients who visit your site with a strong understanding of the problems you solve and the solutions you provide—all reasons for connecting!

<<<<<<<<<<<<<<<<<<<<<<<<<<<<<<<<<<<<<<<

Want more info on creating your content marketing strategies and tactics? Then be sure to check out these bonuses:

Content Marketing Report
http://www.musselwhitemarketing.com/content-marketing-report

Killer Content Marketing Guide
http://www.musselwhitemarketing.com/killer-content-marketing-guide

>>>>>>>>>>>>>>>>>>>>>>>>>>>>>>>>>>>>>>>

Important - Read This:

There are a lot of links to articles, posts, and other resources in this book. Whether you're reading the online version, the soft copy, or the hard copy, we've included all the links in the back of this book in the resource section.

PILLAR #3

E-Mail Marketing for Your Insurance Agency

The reports of death of e-mail marketing have been greatly exaggerated.

Contrary to what some marketers pontificate, e-mail marketing is not dead. In a lot of ways it has gotten stronger. Think about it—while social media might be part of most people's (prospects) daily routine, our job is to move them off of the noisy attention-grabbing channels and create a one-to-one conversation with them. Even if you send an e-mail that they choose not to open and delete, they've at least seen your name and had to think about you for a fraction of second before throwing away the e-mail. This same experience is not guaranteed with any social media channel. One reason being that your posting schedule may not align with your prospects' social media schedule even if they are connected to you.

Let's cut straight to the chase: Ryan Deiss is a master of e-mail marketing. He is the cofounder of Idea Incubator LLP and CEO of DigitalMarketer. com. According to Ryan, he launched his first web-based business from his college dorm room in 1999, and since that time, he has founded over forty different businesses (and been a partner in dozens more) in markets such as health and beauty, survival and preparedness, DIY crafts and home improvement, investing and finance, chemical and liquid-filter manufacturing, business lending, and online skills training and menswear, just to name a few.

In fact, at the time of this writing, Ryan and his team have:

- Invested over *$15 million* in marketing tests
- Generated tens of millions of unique visitors
- Sent well over *a billion* permission-based e-mails
- Run approximately three thousand split and multivariant tests

We share all this simply to say, "We read everything Ryan puts out." Our favorite book on e-mail marketing is Ryan's Invisible Selling Machine and we suggest picking up a copy and reading cover to cover.

Russell Brunson is another brilliant strategist, in our opinion, and the author of DotComSecrets.

Russell is a serial entrepreneur who like Ryan Deiss started his first online company while still in college. Within a year of graduating, Russell sold over a million dollars' worth of his own products and services from his basement!

Russell has a long track record of starting and scaling companies online. He owns a software company, a supplement company, and a coaching company, and is one of the top superaffiliates in the world.

He wrote *DotComSecrets* to help entrepreneurs around the world start, promote, and grow their companies online.

If you think you have a traffic or conversion problem, conversion is rarely the case, according to Russell. Low traffic and weak conversion numbers are just symptoms of a much greater problem, a problem that is a little harder to see (the bad news) but a lot easier to fix (the good news). *DotComSecrets* provides you with the marketing funnels and the sales scripts you need to start attracting new leads to your business.

DotComSecrets offers just the right mix of high-level strategy and low-level tactics to make it a solid playbook for anyone wanting to make his or her online business a profitable one, while operating with the highest degree of ethics and integrity.

We promote Ryan and Russell for their knowledge and results. Together these two authors offer a strong point of view for achieving online success. If you want to improve and increase your website traffic, or convert the visitor traffic when it shows up, these are the guys to study.

There are many reasons why you should focus on building a strong and healthy e-mail list but two of our most important are:

- It will give you a one-to-one communication path with the recipient.
- It can be used to automate several time-consuming tasks, which in turn will make you more efficient and effective.

The Five Phases of E-Mail Marketing

In *Invisible Selling Machine*, Ryan lays out a five-phase formula for e-mail marketing success:

1. **Indoctrination**: Introduce new leads to yourself and your brand, and turn strangers into friends.
2. **Engagement**: Talk to your leads about what interests them and encourage them to buy a relevant product or service.
3. **Ascension**: Welcome your new customers and encourage them to upgrade their experience by purchasing from you again.

4. **Segmentation**: Find out what your clients want to hear more about and what they might want to buy next.
5. **Reengagement**: Bring your customers back when they've fallen out of touch or the relationship has gone cold.

Now before you say or think this won't work for my prospects and clients, remember that Ryan hasn't just tried this formula; he has proven that it works in multiple businesses over and over again. There are no absolutes online, and Ryan's formula is not simply something you can "copy and paste" but rather must be modified and adapted for your audience, but if you can use it effectively the formula is a solid results-generating foundation!

Social media may be in style, but e-mail is where it's at! In other words, e-mail is not dead; far from it actually. E-mail marketing is an opt-in practice, making it a form of "permission marketing." Email marketing can be a super effective consumer-engagement tool that will keep consumers and agency owners connected.

According to numerous reporting agencies, e-mail marketing provides some of the best ROI for businesses of all types:

- E-mail marketing produces an average ROI of $38 for each $1 spent. This is a big increase from the $24.93 ROI reported in 2013.
- One in five companies report an ROI on e-mail marketing of over 70:1.
- E-mail marketing yields an average *4,300 percent ROI* for businesses in the United States (Direct Marketing Association).
- Companies using e-mail to nurture leads generate *50 percent more sales-ready leads* at a *33 percent lower cost*. And nurtured leads, on average, produce a *20 percent increase in sales opportunities* over nonnurtured leads (Hubspot).
- Small business owners estimate that the extra hour that they get back in their day from doing their own e-mail marketing (and other activities) is worth $273/hour (Constant Contact).

- For every $1 spent on e-mail marketing, the average ROI is $44.25 (ExactTarget).
- Marketers consistently ranked e-mail as the *single-most-effective tactic* for awareness, acquisition, conversion, and retention (Gigaom Research).
- E-mail conversion rates are 17 percent, or three times, higher than those of social media (McKinsey & Company)
- Using e-mail is nearly forty times more effective than using Facebook and Twitter for acquiring customers. (McKinsey & Company)
- 70 percent of people say they always open e-mails from their favorite companies (ExactTarget).
- 95 percent of those who opt into e-mail messages from brands find these messages somewhat or very useful (Salesforce).
- You have just three to four seconds to grab your reader's attention and interest him or her enough to open and read your e-mail (Litmus).
- 64 percent of decision makers read e-mails via mobile device (EmailExpert).
- 91 percent of consumers check their e-mail at least once per day on their smart phone, making it the most used functionality (ExactTarget).
- Using marketing automation can increase conversion rates by over 50 percent. (Aberdeen Group).
- Personalized promotional mailings have 29 percent higher unique open rates and 41 percent higher unique click rates than nonpersonalized mailings (Experian).
- Companies that use e-mail list segmentation saw 39 percent higher open rates and 28 percent lower unsubscribe rates (Lyris Annual Email Optimizer Report).
- E-mails with social-sharing buttons increase click-through rates by 158 percent. (Nonprofit Hub).
- The two biggest factors influencing open rates are the organization sending the e-mail (64 percent) and the subject line (47 percent) (Chadwick Martin Bailey).
- If an e-mail does not display correctly, 71.2 percent of people will delete it immediately (BlueHornet).

It's statistics like these that give credence to why smart successful market- ers like Ryan Diess, Russell Brunson, Frank Kern, Mike Filsaime, Andy Jenkins, Amy Porterfield, James Wedmore, and many more have built seven- and eight-figure businesses relying on a strong foundation of e-mail marketing.

When you want to grow your business, acquire new customers, launch a new product, or offer a promotion, you turn to e-mail. Why? Because e-mail delivers better than any other channel, being forty times more effec- tive at acquiring new customers than Facebook or Twitter.

Converting Leads and Gaining Long-Term Customers

In pillar #1, in which we went over your website, I discussed the impor- tance of driving traffic to your site and capturing leads with a custom lead magnet and posting frequently and consistently to your business and per- sonal social media profiles. But as you know, insurance is a contact sport requiring that you get in touch with someone as many as ten to twelve times (if not more) before he or she associates your name with what you provide, yet very few salespeople make more than three calls to follow up. What's more, once a lead is generated, getting an immediate response is crucial to a high close ratio. Are you or your salespeople following up and getting responses?

Your agency strategy should be to leverage social media, local events, and other opportunities to grow your e-mail marketing list and move the conversation from "one to many" on social media to "one to one" with e-mail, using a drip marketing system with your favorite e-mail marketing platform. You will not only be driving traffic through SEO to your website and capturing leads, you'll also be setting up the mechanism to engage, share, and communicate with your prospects automatically.

Once you have your lead magnet in place and leverage your e-mail marketing platform, your online leads will automatically go into your sys- tem so that you can send them follow-up e-mails and build a "know, like, and trust" strategy. With a properly built and leveraged e-mail marketing platform, you can:

- Follow up on leads
- Cross-sale and up-sell
- Renew sales and increase customer retention
- Gain back lapsed customers
- Obtain referrals
- Establish relationships through long-term lead warming

What's more, an e-mail marketing platform will allow you to qualify leads who have received a series of drip e-mails, potentially increasing your connect and conversion rates by five times FROM what you experience with cold calls alone.

With the increasing proliferation of smart phones and tablets, consumers have a veritable traveling inbox, which in turn gives your agency increased access to current and potential clients for pennies per message.

Creating an E-Mail Campaign

E-mail marketing allows your business to easily measure the effectiveness of your current marketing plan. E-mail campaigns give your agency the ability to schedule its outgoing messages so that a certain recipient gets the appropriate information at the appropriate time based on specific time lines (e.g., new clients might get their own newsletters in a certain frequency) or scheduled automation (e.g., Saturday morning safety tips). The e-mails you use in your campaign should be *personalized* with customer names, a unique welcome message, expiration date reminders, and/or personalized product recommendations.

Types of common automated messages include:

- welcoming
- onboarding
- expiration date reminders
- nurturing leads
- holidays
- birthdays
- anniversaries

- recommendations
- renewals
- confirmations
- engagement
- community events
- unsubscribes

It used to be that most insurance agents focused their marketing efforts on mailing letters to the communities they served, advertising in local newspapers, and sponsoring area events. These can still be productive activities and campaigns, but their usefulness and success increase when combined with an e-mail marketing campaign.

As we pointed out earlier, e-mail marketing is the leading tool for increasing market share among independent agents. A recent survey by comScore found that checking and sending e-mail is the most common activity US adults do on their smart phones. Of the 7,400 people surveyed, 78 percent of respondents said they use their smart phone to check e-mail, 73 percent said they used it to browse the Internet, and 70 percent said they used it for Facebook.

The survey also suggests the majority of people are reachable on their smart phones. An estimated 145 million Americans now own one (if not more) of these devices. With so many people reachable anytime and anywhere, it goes without saying that e-mail marketing needs to be part of your overall marketing plan. The following sections contain some ideas that will help you get started with your e-mail marketing campaign if you haven't done so already.

Creating an E-Mail Marketing Plan for Success

E-mail marketing success is achieved by planning, testing, reviewing, modifying, testing, and reviewing, over and over again. It is critical that you first write down your goals and plan of action for you to accomplish them. Here are the steps for your e-mail marketing strategy:

1. *Identify the people who are going to be on your e-mail marketing list.* They might include prospects, existing customers, vendors, and so on.

2. *Determine the purpose of your e-mail.* Is it to tell people about a new service; to offer hints, tips, or advice; or will you be offering a special discount that's available?

3. *Outline your goals.* Do you want to convert a prospect to a customer, get people to sign up for a new promotion, or secure requests for quotes for new policies? You have to know the end goal in order to figure out how to get there.

Determining Your Content

Once you make the decision to set up an e-mail marketing program, you need to develop content that can be sent out on a regular basis. Some good choices of topics for an e-mail coming from an insurance agent include hints, tips, or advice; industry news and stories about the benefits of having adequate insurance coverage; or a recap of your latest offers and news stories involving insurance. In addition to the body of your e-mail, it is important to pay close attention to your subject lines as well as to take the time to test your e-mails before you send them.

If your subject line simply says something like "Adequate Insurance Coverage Has Benefited My Customers," most recipients won't click it. However, if you use a *click-bait* subject line that mentions something off the wall or interesting like "See How Adequate Insurance Coverage Saved Ashley's Life," they will more likely want to open your e-mail and read more.

Because successful insurance agents who use e-mail marketing find it important for their e-mails to clients to stand out, they usually don't send just a plain-text e-mail. They typically *include graphics and other types of visually stimulating aspects in the e-mail.*

However, with these added graphics and HTML coding comes a higher risk of mistakes. Most reputable e-mail marketing platforms around today provide an app that allows you to send a test message to yourself and some friends or coworkers in order to ensure that all of the graphics load correctly and everything shows up the way you envisioned. The application should also include the ability to test a variety of e-mail platforms, such as Gmail, Yahoo, and others. Testing your e-mails before you send them also provides the opportunity to proofread your e-mail an addition time to catch any embarrassing typos or broken web links.

How Often Should You Send E-Mail Messages?

We often hear things like, "I don't want to spam my list by sending e-mails too often." We get it. No one wants to be thought of as a spammer, especially by the very list of people you are working to grow a "trust" and "like" relationship with. There is a delicate balance between spamming your recipients with several e-mails a day and sending so few messages that they forget who you are. If you only send an e-mail once a month, there is a strong chance that you are going to lose your subscribers' interest as well as their immediate awareness of you. On the other hand sending an e-mail every day may be too intrusive.

One or two e-mails every week is usually the maximum you should be sending your clients. However, the number of e-mails you send also depends on the content. If you have important info to share, such as breaking news, the next module in your training, prospects and customers will appreciate knowing that information. If you do not have anything newsworthy or time sensitive to send, don't send an e-mail; it's that simple, doing so will only put a useless e-mail in your client's inbox.

Managing Your E-Mail List

Email list management (or email list hygiene) is one of the least implemented tactics yet most important aspects of e-mail marketing. It's important to keep your contact list healthy and up to date. What this really means is that you should be proactive about *removing inactive non-deliverable contacts* from your list. What's the point of sending out e-mails that no one ever reads?

By maintaining a watchful eye on your email metrics (bounces, clicks, opens, TiNs, etc.) and keeping your sender score (spam complaints, spam traps, unknown users, etc.) at neutral or better, you'll see how your e-mails are being received by subscribers.

Removing contacts from your email marketing list feels counterintuitive, but from a technical standpoint bounces and unopens can damage your deliverability rates and sender reputation. If your deliverability rates drop far enough, your e-mails will be marked as spam and not be delivered.

Most folks don't know what their sender reputation score is. Do you? If not, here are five sites that will help you check your sending reputation and keep you on track:

1. **SenderScore.org:** This site tests and reveals your email marketing sender reputation. Scores are calculated from 0 to 100. The higher your score, the better your reputation and the higher your e-mail deliverability rate. Scores are calculated on a rolling thirty-day average.
2. **Senderbase.org:** This site provides you with the tools to check your sender reputation by ranking you as *Good, Neutral,* or *Poor. Good* means there is little or no threat activity. *Neutral* means your IP address or domain is within acceptable parameters but may still be filtered or blocked. *Poor* means there is a problematic level of threat activity and you are likely to be filtered or blocked.
3. **ReputationAuthority**: This site helps protect businesses from unwanted e-mail and web traffic that contain spam, malware, spyware, malicious code, and phishing attacks. You can look up your IP address or domain, receive a reputation score from 0 to 100, and get the percentage of your e-mails that are good versus bad.
4. **BarracudaCentral:** This site provides both an IP and domain reputation lookup via its Barracuda Reputation System—a real-time database of IP addresses with poor or good reputations.
5. **TrustedSource:** This site is very similar to Senderbase.org, except that it is run by McAfee. It provides information on both your domain's e-mail and web reputations as well as affiliations, domain name system (DNS), and mail server information. It also provides details on the history, activation, and associations of your domain.

Reconfirmation E-Mail Strategy

One way to ensure your contacts are up to date is to send a group reconfirmation e-mail.

If you notice that you get a lot of "bounce-backs"—e-mails sent back to you saying the recipient didn't receive your communication—remove those people from your list and then try to find their most recent e-mail address by calling them or even looking up their LinkedIn profile. You can even Google their name and the word "e-mail" to see what comes up. The fewer number of names that the e-mail has to be sent to, the faster the sending will be. Remove people who no longer want to be included or who have new contact information so you can send your e-mails more quickly to the ones who do want to read them. This also removes the "bloat" of your e-mail list, which could lead to lower costs on your e-mail marketing campaigns.

Creating and sending a group reconfirmation e-mail can be a little in-volved, so we encourage you to do your research and due diligence or hire someone to do it for you correctly.

In our opinion, if you learn *only one* new skill related to success online, it should be e-mail management. Nearly all other technical aspects of your success online can be easily "crowd sourced" or outsourced, but you *must* have a "grow the list" mentality.

Learning the possibilities and automation strategies behind e-mail marketing is something too important to leave in the hands of someone else until you grasp it yourself. It's also extremely inexpensive to learn and manage.

There is no asset more powerful in *any* business than a list of customers who have "signed up," indicating that they want to hear from you. Having as much contact information as possible makes the list even more power-ful. Currently the *most profitable, cheapest, and easiest* way to stay in touch with and grow a relationship with such a contact list is unquestionably via e-mail marketing.

The powerful benefit potential of e-mail marketing is building a con-tact list on autopilot and saving yourself tremendous amounts of time by nurturing your clients and prospects. This will allow you to stay on the top of their minds.

<<<<<<<<<<<<<<<<<<<<<<<<<<<<<<<<<<<<<

The importance of e-mail cannot be stated strongly enough. Therefore, check out these *bonuses*:

Mastering E-Mail Marketing
http://www.MusselwhiteMarketing.com/mastering-email-marketing

E-Mail Marketing Cheat Sheets
http://www.MusselwhiteMarketing.com/email-marketing-cheat-sheets

Invisible Sales Machine
http://www.InvisibleSellingMachine.com/hardcover

Dotcom Secrets
http://www.DotComSecretsBook.com/get-it-free

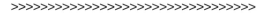

Important - Read This:

There are a lot of links to articles, posts, and other resources in this book. Whether you're reading the online version, the soft copy, or the hard copy, we've included all the links in the back of this book in the resource section.

PILLAR #4

ONLINE ADS FOR YOUR INSURANCE AGENCY

To start this section, we want to make it very clear that while ads are a very real and important strategy in most marketing efforts, they aren't meant to be permanent!

In our opinion, *ads are nothing more than rented attention*. Rented attention isn't necessarily a bad thing. It produces fast results and can be a temporary solution to the problems and challenges of your website not having a strong online presence, an event, a new product service, or something else. Ads or rented attention can be a strong way to kick-start your list-building efforts that we discussed in pillar #3

There are a plethora of strategies and tactics for leveraging ads in your agency's marketing efforts. In the following sections we've provided a cursory review of what's possible.

Using Ads to Increase and Improve Your Agency's Online Visibility and Search Results

Just a couple short years ago we were preaching, "There's no need to pay for ads." A lot has changed!

A lot of insurance agencies still aren't advertising online due to skepticism about paid advertising. Online advertising is not as scary as it once was or is made out to be today. Online advertising also known as Pay per click (PPC) and other paid advertising can be affordable methods to build and increase your agencies awareness. One of the nice things about online advertising it that you have control over your budget and how much you spend each day. You can also segment your target audience by many characteristics, including household income, location, and interests.

For insurance agencies, paid search, or online insurance advertising, has received a reputation as being ineffective and expensive over the years. While this reputation is somewhat accurate, paid search does have a place in many agencies' online marketing strategies. The path to an effective paid search is setting realistic expectations and knowing what you're doing.

Google AdWords for Insurance Agencies

It used to be that paid search referred to Google AdWords exclusively. Now Google AdWords is only one form of online insurance advertising. The service is a somewhat complex auction method in which you bid for your ad to show up alongside, or atop, Google Search results. Because insurance is an expensive word (in 2013, insurance related words accounted for 24 percent of all ads, costing up to more than $50 per click) to bid on, it's something we suggest most agents avoid.

Social Media Advertising

Today, paid search includes alternatives like:

- Google AdWords
- Facebook advertising

- YouTube Advertising
- LinkedIn Advertising
- Twitter Advertising

Online advertising can be a great way to target the exact individuals you want with a very specific ad designed just for them, and at an economical cost.

How would you like to target a personal lines ad to married women in a certain zip code between the ages of thirty and fifty with a household income above $100,000? You can!

How about an ad targeting commercial business to business owners in the field of manufacturing with annual revenues between $10 million and $100 million? You can do that, too!

With targeted ads, it's never been easier to get your agency in front of the right people for a fraction of the cost of what you might expect. Like Facebook, LinkedIn offers advertising options that allow you to target marketing people in certain industries with certain titles or job descriptions, even people that work at certain companies.

Display Ads and Retargeting

Display ads and retargeting are yet other options that can allow your insurance agency to effectively and affordably advertise online. Retargeting, or remarketing, is targeting people who have visited your website (or clicked one of your ads) at some point in the past. If you've ever visited Amazon or eBay, you've probably experienced something you were looking at popping up on other sites and following you around online. That's an example of display ad retargeting. Amazon and eBay are masters at retargeting and remarketing. The idea behind these functions is that when someone shows an interest in a business, product, or service, it takes several viewings before the person decides to move forward with purchasing the product or service and eventually returns to your website.

Today if you want fast results, nothing is faster than online ads, whether on Google, Facebook, YouTube, LinkedIn, Twitter, or another site. The options aren't infinite, but it seems like every day new alternatives are popping up.

Depending on the platform, ads can be a powerful way to reach your target audience skyrocketing the ROI for your business by driving laser-targeted traffic at minimum cost.

Some key benefits of running an online ad campaign include:

- You only pay when someone clicks your ad.
- You can set a daily budget to control your advertising spending.
- Your costs are based on keyword popularity (more popular and competitive keywords cost more).
- You can set geographical constraints and parameters on where your ad will show up. You don't want to pay for clicks by folks that aren't in your target areas.
- People who are searching for your preferred keywords are likely to be more qualified prospects than those you would access with other traditional media.

It is beyond the scope of this book to review and discuss every online advertising platform (e.g., Google, Bing, Facebook, YouTube, etc…) available. Our approach is simply to discuss a cursory strategy that can be implemented across all platforms. Because, when it comes down to it, creating an effective online ad campaign for your agency is all about reaching the right people with the right message at the right time. Consider the consumer or your target audience perspective. online ads, can serve as great reminders to buy that product, opt in to that offer, click that link, etc… They could even show you something you may have otherwise missed. Remember the online attention span dilemma we talked about back in pillar one?

It's our opinion that one of the most flexible and powerful online ad platforms today belongs to Facebook. You can do things with the Facebook Power Editor Ad Platform that you can't do with the other platforms.

And before you say to yourself, "But my clients and prospects aren't on Facebook," take into consideration that according to *USA Today*, most moms and 58 percent of Americans are on Facebook. Facebook is the most popular social media site in the United States. So, while not everyone is on Facebook or social media, we think it is safe to say that a significant amount of your target audience uses Facebook.

While we're big fans of Facebook's online advertising platform, the smart insurance agency (any business really) pays attention to and plays by the rules that Google sets.

Facebook Ad Success Story

We provide marketing services for one of the gyms we're members of, and around the fifteenth of one month, the general manager, Ryan, approached us with the concern that the gym was going to fall short of its new membership goal. We suggested they try a Facebook advertising campaign. The results: by the thirtieth of the month not only did we help them reach their membership goal, they exceeded it by so much that it was one of their best months ever. Since that time we've been running Facebook ads for their new memberships every month.

Obviously a gym isn't the same as an insurance agency, but with the right approach and strategy—know your target audience's and buyers' personas, understand and speak to their pains and challenges, and offer them something of value (like a lead magnet)—an industry agency can also leverage online platforms and the concentration of its target audiences to increase and improve its online visibility.

Depending on the online advertising platform you choose to use, there are types of technology that should be leveraged for maximum results:

- Retargeting pixels
- Conversion pixels
- Customized website audiences
- Look-alike audiences

- Bidding strategies
- Ad duration strategies
- Exclusionary logic
- Multiple ad sets

Online advertising is another area that you can choose to learn on your own, but we suggest you simply find someone with the track record and results you want and invest in his or her service.

<<<<<<<<<<<<<<<<<<<<<<<<<<<<<<<<<<<<<<

Check out these bonus online advertising links:

Pay per Click Made Easy
http://www.Musselwhitemarketing.com/pay-per-click-made-easy

Jon Loomer Link
http://www.Jonloomer.com

>>>>>>>>>>>>>>>>>>>>>>>>>>>>>>>>>>>>>>

Important - Read This:

There are a lot of links to articles, posts, and other resources in this book. Whether you're reading the online version, the soft copy, or the hard copy, we've included all the links in the back of this book in the resource section.

PILLAR #5

Video Marketing for Your Insurance Agency

B efore we get into video marketing, let's consider a few mind-blowing statistics:

- YouTube is the second-most-used search engine in the world.
- One-third of all online activity consists of watching video.
- It is *fifty times easier* to get a page-one ranking on Google when a video is included on your website.
- Three-quarters of all business executives watch work-related videos at least once a week.
- Nearly 60 percent of executives surveyed said they prefer to watch video than to read text.
- Three-fourths of video viewers visit a business's website after watching one of its videos.

- Real estate listings that feature videos generate more than four times the leads of listings without them. This makes a strong argument for using videos for insurance businesses, no?
- When videos are included in e-mails, click-through rates increase by 200–300 percent and opt-out rates decline by 75 percent.
- Only 20 percent of visitors read the entire content of a page on a website, whereas a whopping 80 percent watch videos from start to finish!
- More video content is uploaded onto the web every thirty days than all the content created by ABC, CBS, and NBC in the last thirty years put together!

Of all the insurance agencies and businesses we work with, video is a highly underutilized asset. One of our favorite things about video is that compared to other tactics, you control the frame of reference. And this is critically important, especially when it comes to your insurance marketing strategy. By controlling the experience through video and connecting with your viewer through different modalities—*visual* (seeing), *auditory* (hearing), and *kinesthetic* (moving)—you can influence the way your clients and prospects think, feel, and react to you, your products, and your services.

The fact is that most people are visual learners, and the combination of voice, imagery, and text is more much more engaging than text alone. The opportunity to use video in your agency is such a big opportunity that we could (and probably will) write a book on this topic all by itself. With video, you can show clients and prospects the value of working with you and your agency over any other agency.

With video, you can record messages for clients and prospects once and it can be delivered thousands of times, twenty-four hours a day, 365 days a year, whether it's two in the afternoon or two in the morning.

Contrary to what most video marketers would tell you (we know because we deal with them all the time), every video *does not* need to be a big-lights, big-camera production. If you own an Android or iPhone, you have a legitimate portable studio that records and can produce video good enough for the web. And the best thing is that you probably have your smart phone at your fingertips 24/7 ready to be pulled out and placed into action within seconds.

Here are a few types of videos you can make for your insurance agency:

- client testimonials (more on this topic in pillar #7)
- agency mission statement
- a recorded seminar
- a review of frequently asked questions
- interviews with local business owners residents
- interviews with clients about their experiences after submitting a claim
- welcome-aboard videos
- videos explaining why to work with your agency
- an explanation of types of insurance coverage
- staff member interviews
- an interview a local nonprofit
- a recording of a local community event
- videos of birthdays parties
- videos of anniversary parties
- recordings of holiday events

In addition to some amazing user engagement benefits, video also offers your insurance agency some pretty powerful technical advantages.

Digital Asset with Maximum SEO Benefits

As stated earlier, it is fifty times easier to rank a webpage on Google *when it includes a video.* YouTube isn't the only video platform available and isn't necessarily the best one out there, but as an asset of Google and the second-largest search engine in the world, it's a safe bet that posting and publishing videos on the site will increase and improve your online visibility and searchability.

When posting and publishing to YouTube there are four things you must do in the description accompanying the video:

1. Include a link to your website at the beginning of the text. YouTube cuts off the description after a couple lines and you want viewers to be able to click the link to your site without having to expand the description.
2. Include your agency's name, address, and phone number at the bottom. Having these additional business citations will help your local rankings with search engines.
3. Use the full five thousand characters available in the description field.
4. Include a CTA (call to action), which tell viewers what to do next.

New Video Platforms

With the rise of new video networks, short-form (under 10-minutes) video is poised to trump long-form video (over 10-minutes) and has taken the millennial world by storm and offering some exciting possibilities for the future. Check out these relatively new platforms:

- Periscope
- Meerkat
- Vine
- Snapchat
- Instagram

Making video isn't as time consuming or technical as it used to be and is only going to get easier. Check out these free or low-fee resource tools for making video:

- **Windows Movie Maker**: One of the best free (with Windows) video-editing applications out there and certainly the most popular one on the market.
- **WeVideo**: Cloud-based video editing.
- **iMovie**: Preinstalled on Mac OSs, the (arguably) most user-friendly video creation tool. If you're deciding on a new computer, it's hard

to argue with a passionate Mac user about which provides the best video tool.

- **Final Cut Pro**: is a video editing software from the folks at Apple.
- **Jing**: TechSmith's web-based video/screen capture tool.
- **Screencast**: is another TechSmith solution for businesses looking to manage and share videos, images, documents, or anything else online. Screencast.com's high-quality content-hosting gives you complete control over how, when and to whom your content is distributed.
- **Animoto**: Free for short videos (and you should be keeping your messages short), this web-based service allows you to upload still images or short clips and combine them with royalty-free music.

Using Video to Increase and Improve Your Online Visibility and Search Results

Video is no longer *the secret weapon*; it's simply mandatory if you're look-ing for a marketing differentiator. Make no mistake—every day you wait to incorporate video marketing campaigns leaves the door open for the competition to get ahead of you.

There simply is no other way to put it: Video is hot for businesses right now! YouTube has been the go-to solution for years, but now with alter-native solutions and increased pressure from Facebook, Twitter, Vine, and other platforms, who knows what the preferred platform will be next month or next year? Does it even matter? What matters is that video is at a fast rate becoming the preferred content consumption tool.

Google likes to display a wide variety of media in its search results—including videos. And, as we mentioned earlier, video is 50 percent more likely than a landing page on the same topic to get ranked highly in a search result. We've seen this happen and added video to improve our own and our clients' ranking. Our best result was getting a new video indexed by Google in forty-three minutes.

We are strong believers and proponents of video as rich a media con-tent that can boost customer engagement by holding your website visitors attention longer and possibly converting more sales. When video is implemented creatively, cleverly and with purpose, video can transform your website into a dynamic interactive experience attracting repeat visits.

At the end of the day, as Seth Godin says, "Marketing is a contest for people's attention."

So, having said all that, there's no time like now to start using video in your insurance agency's marketing plan to connect with your current and future clients and to separate yourself from the competition. One warning, however: When it comes to video, most people don't like to see or hear themselves featured. With our years of experience doing video marketing, we've figured out quite a few tricks to combat this this challenge. Just remember: Something done at all is better than something done perfectly, and when it comes to digital marketing (especially video), you can always improve, upgrade, redo…*just get started.*

<<<<<<<<<<<<<<<<<<<<<<<<<<<<<<<<<<<<<<

Will video be your secret weapon?
Check out these bonuses to blow the doors off your marketing potential!

Video Marketing Cheat Sheets
http://www.MusselwhiteMarketing.com/video-marketing-cheat-sheets

Video Marketing Excellence
http://www.MusselwhiteMarketing.com/video-marketing-excellence

>>>>>>>>>>>>>>>>>>>>>>>>>>>>>>>>>>>>>

Important - Read This:

There are a lot of links to articles, posts, and other resources in this book. Whether you're reading the online version, the soft copy, or the hard copy, we've included all the links in the back of this book in the resource section.

PILLAR #6

Social Media Marketing for Your Insurance Agency

I n our first book, *Marketing Online Strategies* (http://www.musselwhite-marketing.com/marketing-online-strategies/) we spent quite a bit of time talking about social media. To cover social media correctly we would end up writing a book on each platform. Obviously we don't have that luxury here. Suffice it to say, there's still a lot of hype surrounding social media, but the reality is that social media is really nothing more than a set of alternative advertising platforms that insurance agencies can take advantage of. At the same time, insurance agencies can and should leverage social media to establish online relationships with prospects, partners and customers.

And with more than 80 percent of American consumers using social media, more and more of them are checking you and your agency out, that could follow up by asking questions or for policy recommendations. With so many folks (potential future customers) using social media on a daily basis, social media should be an integral component of your online marketing strategy. Social Media can be a cost efficient method (compared to alternatives) of making new contacts, staying top of mind with current customers, driving traffic to your website and building your insurance expert reputation.

Just to be clear, even though you currently don't have to pay to use some of the more popular social media platforms, **ALL** social media requires an investment of time (and as we all know, time is money).

Today's successful insurance agencies go where their prospects, customers, and other businesses go to interact, to share, and even to vent. Agencies (yours) need to deliberately and intentionally add their story to their marketing strategy.

When done correctly, the right prospects and future customers will be organically attracted to your story, your brand, your expertise and the things that make you stand out. Social media is a way to accomplish this and it's a powerful and efficient component to leverage your digital footprint, provide you with incredible reach, and bring you front and center to heart of online communication.

Most businesses approach social media incorrectly by posting irrelevant incongruent pictures, videos, and posts. This may feel like a lot of work (because it is) and it's also just not productive. One of the best ways you can use social media is to be a connector, not just an organization that sends out information. Comment on others' posts, profiles, and photos, and reply to their comments about yours. This will help you build a stronger online network. The thing is that your business is about more than just selling insurance; you're a relationship builder. What you essentially do is build relationships with people, and it just so happens that the service you provide is insurance. And that's really what social media is all about—building relationships.

As we discussed in pillar #4, on online advertising, social media isn't just for millennials anymore. The adoption rate by more mature users is soaring. According to a 2014 Facebook Demographics Report, its biggest segment for growth has been the fifty-five-plus age group. Facebook has opened the doors for all age groups to connect with friends and family and keeping themselves in the loop on contemporary news and world events. The site can be a great way to connect with your customers. Its popularity means that many of your prospects and customers are already using it to keep in touch not only with family and friends but also with companies.

LinkedIn is another popular social network for the more mature generation, accounting for more than half of Internet users overall. LinkedIn is a social network for business professionals on which members create detailed personal profiles much like a resume. The site also offers online groups of individuals who share common interests and goals. By participating in these groups in the discussion forums, you can post and publish news about your products and services. Many LinkedIn users have embraced social media for the power it holds as they shifted careers and pursued their passions. Today however a lot of businesses use LinkedIn as an online database providing all sorts of incite on prospects of all sorts.

Twitter has the least number of older users, with only 18 percent of users reporting that they are over the age of fifty; in that age group, most use it to find health information, follow news outlets, and literary publications.

YouTube is attracting a growing percentage of older users, with the largest demographic in the forty-five to fifty-four age bracket, followed closely by those ages fifty-five to sixty-four.

So, the older generation *is* using social media. Although their use is mainly to connect with family, many are now using it to look for news and information as well as ratings for businesses, products, and services. Not only is this age group highly engaged, it also has forty-seven times the net worth of households thirty-five and older.

What does all this mean for insurance agency owners?

Insurance agencies shouldn't ignore this important demographic and the growth it has experienced with using online media. Remember, "Every day for the next two decades, 10,000 boomers will join in the marketing wasteland of 'seniors." (Carmichael, Matt. "Marketing wasteland Clermont, Fla., May 28, 2012). At the very least, agencies need to start understanding and capitalizing on social media marketing toward older citizens—a demographic that is becoming more computer literate than any senior generation before.

Regardless of the demographic, social media can be a powerful tool (when you correctly and with a strategy) for reaching the masses.

Managing Your Social Media Presence

Like any business initiative, good management is key to long-term success. Social networking is no different. Think back to when you purchased your agency's first automation system—success relied on rethinking how your business would be run and putting a team in place who would possess the skills necessary to leverage the new technology. Initially, didn't it feel a little awkward? We bet there might have even been a time or two when you questioned the value of the decision to automate. However, we're also betting that today the automation system is foundational to your agency's daily success.

As previously highlighted, social networking is more than just a marketing tool. Sales, customer service, support, claims, and risk management can all benefit from a comprehensive social networking strategy. To that end, it is smart to engage people from all agency disciplines (management, customer service, legal, IT, etc.) in the process of planning, creating strategy, implementing, and participating in your company's social networking initiative.

The value you will gain from social networking will not only affect the way you communicate with your customers; it can also change the way you advertise, provide service, manage relationships, and perhaps even sell products and services.

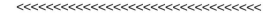

Check out this social media marketing bonus:

Grow Your Business with Social Media
http://www.musselwhitemarketing.com/
grow-your-business-with-social-media

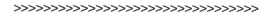

Important - Read This:

There are a lot of links to articles, posts, and other resources in this book. Whether you're reading the online version, the soft copy, or the hard copy, we've included all the links in the back of this book in the resource section.

PILLAR #7

REVIEWS AND TESTIMONIALS FOR YOUR INSURANCE AGENCY

W ord of mouth (marketing) has always been a powerful way to influence business results. Today however consumer opinion travels faster and further than ever before. Since 1991 the world wide web, search engines, social media and an almost countless number of growing review sites have (and continue) to evolve into a medium by which traditional "word of mouth" is broadcast globally; shared easily; and never, ever forgotten.

Numerous studies can be found online revealing that US consumers who have had poor service interactions in the past month, almost a quarter (and growing) have taken to online to vent and share their reviews via Facebook, Twitter, blog posts, etc... and even video. Another study compared the reach of negative and positive comments about businesses and found that on average, unhappy customers tell twenty-four other people, while happy customers tell just fifteen.

Reviews and testimonials (forms of social credibility) are accelerating in popularity. Most folks will jump on their smart phones to look at restaurant reviews, books reviews, local business service reviews, and, yes, even your agency's reviews. By the time prospects have completed their research and due diligence, before even talking to anyone at your agency, typically 60 percent of their purchase decision has already been made.

Today online customer reviews are arguably the greatest influence in attracting and retaining customers for small and local businesses including insurance agencies. Online reviews are growing in popularity helping consumers determine how people perceive a business, which can have a direct impact on whether or not they would buy from it. Online reviews are also starting to have an impact on a businesses (your agency) visibility in search engines.

Today we live in what Forrester Research has dubbed "the age of the customer." Online access at the tip of our fingertips empowers consumers who are more demanding than ever. Online consumers have the ability to make or break your business. They've learned marketing is suspect and not to blindly trust what you say about your product or service. Instead, they trust other people like themselves and the comments and reviews they leave.

It's no secret trust in online reviews is on the rise. According to Nielsen's 2012 *Global Trust in Advertising* survey, 70 percent of consumers trust online reviews from people they don't know.

Around the world over ninety percent of consumers trust word-of-mouth recommendations, whether from strangers or from friends and family.

So, what does this mean for your agency? Ultimately, as an insurance agency operating as a local business, the goal is to rank higher than the competition in local search results. According to Google, three factors influence Google's local search rankings: **relevance** (matches search), **distance**, and **prominence** (how popular your business is). Google takes reviews from many different online sites into consideration (including Yelp, Facebook, and Google), which all influence the rankings you get on a Google local search.

The next time a prospect starts his or her research and due diligence you want your agency to show up as a potential solution for whatever insurance problem they're having or need to address.

Reviews Help You Stand Out

We've shown that collecting online reviews can help your agency rank higher on organic (including local) search results. What follows from this—perhaps obviously—is that online reviews will help your business stand out from the crowd.

Brightlocal (http://www.brightlocal.com) conducted a study in 2014 revealing that the American consumer is increasingly using local reviews to help make purchasing decisions. Their survey shows that 88 percent of consumers use, at least occasionally, local online reviews during the buying decision process.

The bottom line is that online reviews are an important tool for consumers to judge the quality of a business. In the insurance industry there is currently a large opportunity for agencies to stand out on the web. But the vast majority of insurance agencies have at most one or two reviews posted. Many have none at all.

Put yourself in the shoes of a consumer searching online for insurance. When you search online for a product or service we bet you're positively influenced by search results offering a handful of positive reviews? Research and a little commonsense goes a long way online and publishing reviews online can provide social credibility, which impacts purchase decisions.

You probably already have customers that know, like, and trust you. If you haven't already sought their reviews in meaningful published ways, now is the time to start.

The endorsements of happy customers are some of the best and most powerful advertising available to you. Don't miss the opportunity to have happy customers share and promote your agency!

<<<<<<<<<<<<<<<<<<<<<<<<<<<<<<<<<<<<<<

Because your online reputation is too important to ignore, check out these tools:

Online Reputation Assessment Guide
http://www.Musselwhitemarketing.com/
online-reputation-assessment-guide

Rocket Referrals
http://www.rocketreferrals.com

Grade.us
http://www.grade.us

>>>>>>>>>>>>>>>>>>>>>>>>>>>>>>>>>>>>>>>

Important - Read This:

There are a lot of links to articles, posts, and other resources in this book. Whether you're reading the online version, the soft copy, or the hard copy, we've included all the links in the back of this book in the resource section.

Summary

W e've covered a ton of stuff in this book (a lot of it with some degree of technical challenge); arguably maybe even an over-whelming amount. But when it comes to digital marketing, it's our opinion that there are no absolutes, as things are always changing if not accelerating. There aren't any exact sciences to digital marketing success, regardless of what the experts might say.

Our approach has been that success is pursued and attained when focus is placed on the wants, needs, and desires of your customers and prospects, not on your business. In other words, it doesn't really matter what we want, what you want, or what worked last time; what matters most is what motivates your current (best) and future clients to action. These are the things that should determine your focus and the order of those digital marketing activities that provide the best return on investment.

The glue that makes this all work is *getting started* and *getting started with a plan*; specifically a twelve- to eighteen-month content and event calendar (plan). We share a simple formula to make this task super simple. The twelve-four-fifty-two formula simply suggests that having twelve main topics with four supporting topics will net fifty-two weeks of content and activities. We know the formula isn't exact, but you get the concept.

If you apply our plan and consistently follow the tactics outlined in the previous chapters, within a sixty- to ninety-day span you will have made some tremendous progress and should start to see some improvements. If you keep at it consistently and for long enough, you will start to see more improvements, and eventually you'll start to achieve the goals you've been trying to attain (phones ringing, customers expanding, premiums increasing, and ultimately higher revenue and profits).

Again, we know we shared a lot of strategies and tactics in this book. Our goal hasn't been to overwhelm you but to move you to action. You may be wondering where you start or what specifically to do to achieve the results you want. We can help, and we make ourselves available to discuss your specific situation and agency. If you're interested we offer strategy sessions (more like a mini marketing plan) to review and discuss a custom solution for your agency.

Who are Charles and Linda?

It was a terrifyingly exciting leap of faith when we decided to launch our first online venture back in 2008. It took ten years of talking, mulling, and dreaming before we finally decided to pull the trigger and put things into motion, but it took the perfect storm to finally push us over the edge.

First, the bottom dropped out of the economy. Pair that with the fact that we had a major medical hurdle in our family at the time. Mix all of that into a stew pot of good ol' family issues that wouldn't be appropriate to share here, and the result is—we needed *to take action*, or boil alive.

During our time in the corporate world, we had the opportunity to work with many entrepreneurs and small business owners, and we were intrigued by their ability to call their own shots and make their own decisions. We wanted the freedom to both fail and succeed on our own merits and efforts.

We were done with working our butts off for someone else, only to be rewarded at the end of the year with a $1-an-hour raise, which never amounted to much. Do the math: a $1-an-hour raise that equals $2,080 before taxes after you pay taxes on it earns you about two additional visits to the grocery store. Not very appealing, to say the least! We were done with having to ask a friend to do us a favor and spend time with our kids while we went on vacation. To us, it was more about more about freedom and dignity than the money. It was about carving our own path in our own way.

We had no earthly idea of what we were doing when we started. Almost immediately we realized we didn't know what we didn't know.

Fear and doubt set in. We thought we would we lose our home, our cars, our marriage, our kids. It was scary but we weren't going to give up and throw in the towel. We didn't know much about marketing, social media, video marketing, e-mail automation, list building, or any of those other buzzwords and marketing jargon. We didn't even know how to handle the bare-bones basics such a setting up a website. WordPress might as well have been a turn-of-the century printing company for all we knew.

In order to get started, we went the same route a lot of other folks did—we spent an absurd amount of money on every guru, expert, master, and sworn disciple of the gods of marketing we could find. Then, by the grace of God, we met Starr Hall.

Starr had a successful background in PR and was launching a social media certification course that we thought we'd benefit from. So we enrolled and at the completion of the course, Starr approached us and asked if we'd partner with her and handle some of her social media while she was on the road and touring with *Entrepreneur* magazine and American Express Open. This arrangement quickly turned into us also doing the social media marketing for some of her clients. Starr would write the plans and we would execute them from the privacy and convenience of our home office.

For a brief stint we ran our own online business, applying all the strategies and tactics we had learned. We were selling an MLM product but doing it online. A few months into it we were approached by someone from the corporate world who wanted to know what we were doing. We thought to ourselves, Here comes the payday! Instead, the person asked us to stop doing what we were doing because we were messing up the results they were getting for the lots (we assume) of money they were spending. It was at this moment and the culmination of our OJT education that we got our lightbulb and aha moment, telling us that we could and should do this for ourselves and eventually others.

Over time, through trial and error, and by simply learning the results of getting started, we developed a pretty-good system to help entrepreneurs and small businesses get organized, create and implement marketing efforts, and *take action* consistently.

We want to be clear, however: We don't think of ourselves as gurus, experts, or rockstars but simply as students of marketing. We spend lots of time, effort and money every month to stay on top of what's working, what isn't, and what's coming up. We partner with, follow, and are mentored by the top people in our industry.

It's our belief that *attaining success* is our responsibility and duty. We wish we could say we came up with that line, but we picked it up from our friend, mentor, author, and business coach, Grant Cardone. We take this belief a step further in saying that attaining success is all our responsibility.

Success is your responsibility and it's our responsibility. It's our responsibility to one another, our families, our friends, our partners, our employees, and all the communities in which we participate. People are waiting for both of us to show up and solve a problem they are having. So, whether you are selling a product or service, plumbing fittings, coaching, or setting up multimillion dollar computer systems, someone is looking for what you have to offer. Don't let them down. Show up and show up strong. Remember, *Success is your duty.*

If a husband-and-wife team can start a marketing business with zero knowledge of how to do it during a terrible economic crash after years of working in the comfy, drone-like atmosphere of the corporate world, then you most certainly can achieve business success, too. We are now operating a full-service marketing and consulting agency with a team of over twenty and you can to where we are also.

We've talked to a lot of smart, wealthy entrepreneurs and business owners who say it is lonely at the top, which tells us there is still room for both of us up there. Let's get on it!

We look forward to meeting you.

Charles and Linda Musselwhite

http://www.MusselwhiteConsulting.com

Contact@MusselwhiteMarketing.com

Resources

The links below are provided for convenience and informational purposes only; they do not constitute an endorsement or an approval by Musselwhite Marketing Consulting of any of the products, services, or opinions offered. Musselwhite Marketing Consulting bears no responsibility for the accuracy, legality, or content of external sites or for that of subsequent links. Contact the site for answers to questions regarding its content.

Introduction

The zero moment of truth: https://www.thinkwithgoogle.com/collections/zero-moment-truth.html

Online marketing kick-start tips: www.musselwhitemarketing.com/online-marketing-tips-kickstart/

Why digital marketing for your insurance agency (AdAge): http://adage.com/article/special-report-american-consumer-project/marketing-wasteland-clermont-fla/234998/

Pillar #1: Your Insurance Agency Website

Google Search Console Help: https://support.google.com/webmasters/answer/66359?hl=en

Yoast Duplicate Content: Causes and Solutions: https://yoast.com/duplicate-content

Raven Tools: 10 Duplicate Content Scenarios and How to Solve Them - https://raventools.com/blog/resolve-duplicate-content-issues

Search Engine Land: 29 percent of Sites Face Duplicate Content Issues - http://searchengineland.com/study-29-of-sites-face-duplicate-content-issues-80-arent-using-schema-org-microdata-232870

Search Engine Roundtable: How Do You Detect Duplicate Content Issues - https://www.seroundtable.com/google-duplicate-content-seo-20726.html

SEO Site Checkup: The Truth About Duplicate Content Issues - http://seosite-checkup.com/articles/the-truth-about-duplicate-content-issues-in-seo

MOZ: What is Duplicate Content - https://moz.com/learn/seo/duplicate-content

WooRank - www.woorank.com

WooRank expert - https://experts.woorank.com/en/experts/charles-musselwhite

Title tag - http://blog.woorank.com/2014/07/15-title-tag-optimization-guidelines-usability-seo

Most important keywords - http://blog.woorank.com/2014/07/15-title-tag-optimization-guidelines-usability-seo

Meta description - http://blog.woorank.com/2014/07/15-title-tag-optimization-guidelines-usability-seo

Most important keywords - http://blog.woorank.com/2013/09/keyword-strategy-identify-measure-repeat

Online Broken Link Checker - http://www.brokenlinkcheck.com

Dead Link Checker - http://www.deadlinkchecker.com

W3C Link Checker - https://validator.w3.org/checklink

Google Search Console - https://www.google.com/webmasters/tools/home

Bobots.txt file - http://blog.woorank.com/2013/04/robots-txt-a-beginners-guide

Sitemap's location - http://blog.woorank.com/2014/05/how-to-create-a-robots-txt-file-with-sitemap-location

Second-hand domain name - https://sedo.com/us

Image Optimizer - http://www.imageoptimizer.net/Pages/Home.aspx

Optimizilla - http://optimizilla.com

effective alternative text - http://blog.woorank.com/2013/01/image-alt-text-relevant-for-seo-and-usability

Google Images - https://images.google.com

Consistent with your use of keywords - http://blog.woorank.com/2013/02/how-to-maintain-keyword-consistency

25 and 70 percent is ideal - http://blog.woorank.com/2013/03/are-text-to-html-ratios-important

Content is relevant - http://blog.woorank.com/2013/01/6-seo-tips-for-website-content

XML sitemap - https://www.woorank.com/en/p/xml-sitemaps

Building backlinks - http://blog.woorank.com/2013/03/how-to-build-links-to-your-inner-pages

Crawl and index - http://blog.woorank.com/2013/05/11-steps-to-get-your-site-indexed-on-google

Google Search Console - https://www.google.com/webmasters/tools/home

Siteliner - www.siteliner.com

Copyscape - www.copyscape.com

PlagSpotter - www.plagspotter.com

Pass value from one page to another - https://www.woorank.com/en/p/link-juice

Nofollow - http://blog.woorank.com/2013/03/how-can-you-use-the-nofollow-attribute-to-your-advantage

Important factor - http://blog.woorank.com/2014/06/useful-loading-time-measurement-apps

For tips - https://developers.google.com/speed

Website monitoring services - http://blog.woorank.com/2014/05/50-free-uptime-monitoring-services

Uptime Robot - http://uptimerobot.com

Monitor.us - http://www.monitor.us

Montastic - http://www.montastic.com

Site24x7 - http://www.site24x7.com

Service Uptime - http://www.serviceuptime.com

PageSpeed Insights - https://developers.google.com/speed/pagespeed/insights

WebPageTest - http://www.webpagetest.org

Google's 200 Ranking Factors: The Complete List - http://backlinko.com/google-ranking-factors

Rich Snippets - http://blog.woorank.com/2012/12/rich-snippets-what-why-and-how-to-implement

Rich snippets - https://developers.google.com/structured-data/rich-snippets

Reviews - https://developers.google.com/structured-data/rich-snippets/reviews

People - http://schema.org/Person

Products - https://developers.google.com/structured-data/rich-snippets/products

Businesses and Organizations - http://schema.org/Organization

Recipes - https://developers.google.com/structured-data/rich-snippets/recipes

Events - https://developers.google.com/structured-data/rich-snippets/events

Videos - https://developers.google.com/structured-data/rich-snippets/videos

Music - http://schema.org/MusicRecording

Schema.org - http://schema.org/docs/gs.html

Microdata - https://developers.google.com/structured-data/schema-org

Crucial to SEO - http://blog.woorank.com/2013/02/backlinking-factors-to-improve-site-seo

Social media profiles - http://blog.woorank.com/2012/12/social-media-optimization-tips-for-local-seo

Facebook - https://www.facebook.com/pages/create.php

Twitter - https://twitter.com

LinkedIn - https://www.linkedin.com

Google+ - https://plus.google.com

Learn - http://blog.woorank.com/2013/02/7-social-media-tips-to-improve-fan-engagement

Engage - http://blog.woorank.com/2013/04/5-innovative-facebook-marketing-ideas-for-small-businesses

Use your website - http://blog.woorank.com/2012/11/tools-tips-for-integrating-social-media-into-your-website

Hootsuite - https://hootsuite.com

SproutSocial - http://sproutsocial.com

CrowdBooster - http://crowdbooster.com

Google Developers Mobile-Friendly Test - https://www.google.com/webmasters/tools/mobile-friendly

Duda - https://www.dudamobile.com

Mobify - http://www.mobify.com

Wirenode - http://www.wirenode.com

Mippin - http://www.mippin.com/web/maker/mobilize.jsp?from=blog&new=1
Onbile - http://www.onbile.com
Winksite - https://winksite.com/site/index.cfm
Mofuse - http://mofuse.com
LOCAL SEO CHECKLIST - http://www.musselwhitemarketing.com/local-seo-checklist
WEBSITE DESIGN REPORT- www.musselwhitemarketing.com/website-design-report

Pillar #2: Content Marketing for Your Insurance Agency

Content Marketing Institute - http://contentmarketinginstitute.com
Dan Kennedy - http://www.dankennedyonline.com/bio.html
CNN Money - money.cnn.com/pf/insurance
Daily Finance - dailyfinance.com/category/insurance
Bank Rate - bankrate.com/insurance.aspx
Main Street - mainstreet.com/topic/moneyinvesting/insurance
Smart Money - smartmoney.com/personal-finance/insurance
Kiplinger - kiplinger.com/insurance
Motley Fool - fool.com/insurancecenter
Financial Times - ft.com/personal-finance/insurance
New York Times - topics.nytimes.com/your-money/insurance/index.html
New York Times - nytimes.com/pages/health/index.html
WSJ—(Health Blog) - blogs.wsj.com/health
Time—(Healthland) - healthland.time.com
National Association of Insurance Commissioners - naic.org/newsroom.htm
Insurance Information Institute - iii.org/insuranceindustryblog
The Life & Health Insurance Foundation for Education - lifehappens.org/blog
HealthCare.Gov Blog - healthcare.gov/blog
National Institutes of Health - newsinhealth.nih.gov
National Highway Safety Traffic Administration - nhtsa.gov
Insurance Institute For Highway Safety - iihs.org
AAA Safety News - newsroom.aaa.com/safety
Insurance Journal - insurancejournal.com/news

Property Casualty 360 Risk - propertycasualty360.com/Risk

Property Casualty 360 Claims - propertycasualty360.com/Claims

Business Insurance - businessinsurance.com

Life Health Pro - lifehealthpro.com

Claims Journal - claimsjournal.com

Risk and Insurance - riskandinsurance.com

About.com Business Insure - businessinsure.about.com

About.com Insurance - insurance.about.com

Workers Comp Insider - workerscompinsider.com

Winzer Insurance - winzerinsurance.com

Consumer Insurance Blog - insureinfoblog.com

Content Marketing Report - www.musselwhitemarketing.com/content-marketing-report

Pillar #3: E-Mail Marketing for Your Insurance Agency

Invisible Selling Machine - http://invisiblesellingmachine.com/hardcover

Reported in 2013 - http://www.emailmonday.com/dma-national-client-email-report-2015

ROI of over 70:1 - http://www.emailmonday.com/dma-national-client-email-report-2015

Direct Marketing Association - http://www.copyblogger.com/email-marketing

Hubspot - http://www.hubspot.com/marketing-statistics

Constant Contact - http://news.constantcontact.com/research/9162013-small-business-owners-express-desire-outsource-social-media-and-other-marketing-act

ExactTarget - http://www.exacttarget.com/blog/50-email-marketing-tips-and-stats-for-2014

Gigaom Research - http://go.extole.com/rs/extole/images/Gigaom%20Research%20-%20Work%20horses%20and%20dark%20horses.pdf

McKinsey & Company - http://www.mckinsey.com/insights/marketing_sales/why_marketers_should_keep_sending_you_emails

Salesforce - http://blogs.salesforce.com/company/2014/11/75-digital-marketing-stats-from-salesforce-marketing-cloud-research.html

Litmus - https://litmus.com/blog/8-email-design-factors-influence-action

E-mailExpert - http://emailexpert.org/infographic-10-must-know-email-mar-keting-stats-2014

Aberdeen Group - http://aberdeen.com/research/7603/ra-marketing-lead-management/content.aspx

Experian - http://press.experian.com/United-States/Press-Release/experi-an-marketing-services-study-finds-personalized-emails-generate-six.aspx

Lyris Annual E-Mail Optimizer Report - http://www.fulcrumtech.net/wp-content/uploads/2012/10/Lyris-Annual-Email-Optimizer-Report.pdf

NonprofitHub-http://www.nonprofithub.org/nonprofit-marketing-plan/20-marketing-stats-trends-2015

Chadwick Martin Bailey - http://blog.cmbinfo.com/in-the-news-content-/bid/76542/Brand-and-Subject-Lines-Fuel-Email-Opens-Clutter-Drives-Users-Away

BlueHornet - http://resources.bluehornet.com/resources/form/2014-consumer-views-of-email-marketing-report

TiNs - https://sesblog.amazon.com/blog/tag/TiNS

SenderScore.org - https://senderscore.org

Senderbase.org - http://www.senderbase.org

ReputationAuthority - http://www.reputationauthority.org

BarracudaCentral - http://www.barracudacentral.org/lookups

TrustedSource - http://www.trustedsource.org

Mastering E-mail Marketing - MusselwhiteMarketing.com/mastering-email-marketing

E-Mail Marketing Cheat Sheets - MusselwhiteMarketing.com/email-marketing-cheat-sheet

Invisible Sales Machine - InvisibleSellingMachine.com/hardcover

DOTCOM Secrets - DotComSecretsBook.com/get-it-free

Pillar #4: Online Ads for Your Insurance Agency

Insurance is an expensive word - https://searchenginewatch.com/sew/news/2095210/google-makes-billions-expensive-adwords-keyword-cat-egories

Facebook advertising - https://www.facebook.com/advertising

YouTube advertising - https://www.youtube.com/yt/advertise

LinkedIn advertising - https://www.linkedin.com/advertising
Twitter Advertising - https://ads.twitter.com
LinkedIn offers advertising options - http://www.linkedin.com/advertising
58% of Americans are on Facebook - http://www.usatoday.com/story/tech/2015/01/09/pew-survey-social-media-facebook-linkedin-twitter-instagram-pinterest/21461381

Pillar #5: Video Marketing for Your Insurance Agency
Periscope - https://www.periscope.tv
Meerkat - http://meerkatapp.co
Vine - https://vine.co
Snapchat - https://www.snapchat.com
Instagram - https://www.instagram.com
Windows Movie Maker - http://windows.microsoft.com/en-us/windows/get-movie-maker-download
Wevideo - https://www.wevideo.com
Avidemux - http://fixounet.free.fr/avidemux
VSDC Free Video Editor - http://www.videosoftdev.com/free-video-editor
iMovie - http://www.apple.com/ilife/imovie/what-is.html
Lightworks - https://www.lwks.com
Freemake Video Converter - http://www.freemake.com/free_video_converter
Jing - http://www.techsmith.com/jing-features.html
Animoto - http://animoto.com
Video Marketing Cheat Sheets -
http://www.MusselwhiteMarketing.com/video-marketing-cheat-sheets
Video Marketing Excellence -
http://www.MusselwhiteMarketing.com/video-marketing-excellence

Pillar #6: Social Media Marketing for Your Insurance Agency
2014 Facebook Demographics Report - http://www.ibtimes.com/facebook-gets-older-demographic-report-shows-3-million-teens-left-social-network-3-years-1543092
Facebook - https://www.facebook.com

LinkedIn - https://www.linkedin.com
Twitter - https://twitter.com
YouTube - https://www.youtube.com
Grow Your Business With Social Media - http://www.musselwhitemarketing.com/grow-your-business-with-social-media/

Pillar #7: Reviews and Testimonials for Your Insurance Agency

Online Reputation Assessment Guide - https://www.musselwhitemarketing.com/online-reputation-assessment-guide
ROCKET REFFERALS - www.rocketreferrals.com
GRADE.US - www.grade.us

Printed in Great Britain
by Amazon